CW01551693

HISTORY OF BRITAIN

Michael Coombe

UPFRONT PUBLISHING
LEICESTERSHIRE

HISTORY OF BRITAIN
Copyright © 2000 Michael Coombe

ISBN 1 84426 093 3

First Published 2000 by
MINERVA PRESS

Second Edition 2002 by
UPFRONT PUBLISHING
Leicestershire

HISTORY OF BRITAIN

*By kind permission of the headmaster
of St Piran's School, Maidenhead,
and of the Owen family of Llanidloes,
this book is dedicated to the memory of
Cecil Edward Vaughan Owen (1901-1981)
who inspired a love of history
in so many children.*

Contents

Preface

This history book is based on the teaching notes of Cecil Owen to whom it is dedicated. When he retired he left me his notes, and for some years I used them before in my turn passing most of them on to my successor at St Piran's School. I have long thought that they deserved publishing in a form suitable for the age group eleven to thirteen which he taught so successfully for so many years, and indeed for other ages. I feel also that there is an increasing tendency to make children specialise and choose a period for their studies before they have an overall perspective of their country's history. This book, then, which is only an outline history of Britain, will have achieved its object if it leads children of all ages to ask questions and if possible go and look for the answers themselves. My thanks go in particular to Miss Ann Hay and Mrs Marian Lake for all the work they have done in reading and correcting the text and to Mr S L Edginton for checking the wording. The photographs are by kind permission of Mr Peter Coombe.

Chapter I
EARLY TIMES

The story of our country begins many thousands of years ago, long before Britain became an island. It is the story of people moving across Europe because of pressure on their numbers in the east. First they attacked, then they settled. When they arrived they would have found, in the east, level shelving ground from the sea leading to wet, fen-like land, but in the south the shore gave way to the low hills known as the Downs. These areas were covered in low scrub and forest, pierced by rivers easy to sail along. The rivers led into the inland areas, soon to be cultivated by early man. Wild animals roamed the hills and valleys. Many of these animals are no longer seen in Britain. The land was green, fertile and a source of wealth to those who settled. The climate was mild and wet, then, as now, due to the influence of the Gulf Stream. There was plenty of fresh water and timber and the introduction of the plough made the land fruitful. Small groups of people settled by streams and on the upland areas, the origins of our village system.

For thousands of years tribes moved into southern and eastern England attacking those already here and slowly driving them towards the mountains of Wales and Scotland and into Cornwall. As each wave invaded, so those in the coastal areas either submitted or went north and west.

We know something about these neolithic – new Stone Age – men. They tended to be small and dark and were living here when Stonehenge was built. They were driven into what we now call Wales by early Bronze Age people who reconstructed Stonehenge sometime between 1700 and 1500 BC. These people traded far and wide. Egyptian beads have been found in England and English jet in Spain. Copper and tin lay near the surface, especially in Cornwall. When smelted together these minerals became bronze and replaced stone implements. These tribes were very proficient in the use of bronze and, later, tin. The Bronze Age people flourished until the arrival of the Celts during the seventh century BC. They had moved across Europe in various directions. They settled in the region of modern Paris, overran Rome in about 387 BC, invaded Spain and crossed the Channel, imposing themselves on the southern part of the island and once again driving the then inhabitants into the west and south-west.

Estimates of the population of the British Isles in the century before the arrival of the Romans vary, but less than a million seems to be generally agreed. The Celts were tribesmen. They did not have boundaries as we understand them now and their leaders were the local chieftains. The most advanced of these tribes lived in the south-east, where the best grain land was and where communications with Europe were easy. We know little of their religion, except that this was the period of the Druids, who seem to have evolved a religion of fear for their people. It was against these people that Julius Caesar carried out the first of his invasions in 55 BC.

The Romans had conquered the countries round the Mediterranean and most of Gaul – modern France. Julius Caesar wanted to overawe the Celtic inhabitants of Britain because he had evidence that they were sending help to their relatives in France in their struggle against him. Thus he crossed the Straits of Dover with two legions in 55 BC and landed somewhere near Deal. His stay was short because autumn was approaching and he heard of a general revolt in France, so he recrossed the Straits. The next year he came again with a much larger force, twenty-five thousand infantry and two thousand cavalry, and marched into the interior, but a Channel storm disabled many of his ships and he returned to the coast. The chief of the local tribe, the Catuvellauni, a man called Cassivellaunus, gathered together his tribe and others, but Caesar crossed the Thames somewhere near London Bridge and took the town of Verulamium (St Albans). Cassivellaunus and many of the chiefs promised hostages and tribute money to Caesar and so he returned to Gaul.

These promises were not kept, nor could Caesar enforce them as he was concerned with problems in Italy and was murdered in

Rome in 44 BC. In AD 43 Claudius Caesar sent Aulus Plautius to invade and conquer Britain as it was thought this would be of considerable economic advantage to Rome. This was the beginning of a military occupation which lasted nearly four hundred years. Plautius conquered the south-east and took Colchester. Soon after, the ruling chief of that area, Caractacus, was captured and sent to Rome. Claudius himself visited Britain and stayed sixteen days.

The conquest continued slowly and by the year AD 60 had reached Anglesey, the sacred home of the Druids. In that year, when the governor, Suetonius Paulinus, was in the island, the queen of the Iceni tribe, Boudicca, led a rebellion. She had been very badly treated by Roman officials and called on the Britons to come to her help. In a short and rapid campaign, she burnt London, St Albans and Colchester and destroyed a Roman legion. Paulinus hurried back from Anglesey and met Boudicca near Colchester. Boudicca was heavily defeated and poisoned herself soon after. Paulinus was recalled to Rome.

By AD 78 most of Britain had been conquered, and in AD 122 the Roman emperor of the time, Hadrian, visited the island and ordered the building of a stone wall from Carlisle to Newcastle, garrisoned by soldiers drawn from various parts of the empire.

The conquest was pushed further north and a turf wall was built between the Forth and Clyde by Antoninus, and in the year AD 208 Severus visited the island and strengthened this earthwork.

During this period Christianity had come with the soldiers and merchants, and in AD 305 St Alban was martyred. The year after Constantine was proclaimed emperor of Rome in Britain. He was to be the first Christian emperor.

Towards the end of the third century, Rome began to decline, coming under attack from invaders on its northern borders and the Saxons began their attacks on the east coast of Britain. By 410 Rome was very hard pressed and so withdrew its troops from Britain; the occupation was over but not the effects and results.

For a period of nearly four hundred years Britain had been under the control of Rome and we should look at some of the results of this occupation. Many fine roads were built, not to be bettered until the nineteenth century. These enabled the Romans to move troops quickly about the country.

Britain, for the first time, was given strong government and a system of laws. We can see the remains of villas, baths and amphitheatres and so know the high state of civilisation the Romans reached. Iron, lead, gold and tin mines were extensively worked and such quantities of grain produced that Britain was known as the 'Granary of the North'. Large towns came into existence for the first time, such as London, Bath and St Albans, and Christianity was introduced into the country.

The period from the Roman evacuation to the Norman Conquest is over six hundred years. It begins with the Saxon invasions and the English settlements. These tribes, the Saxons, Angles and Jutes, came from south Denmark and north Germany and settled in Kent, Sussex and East Anglia.

We shall be mainly concerned with the Saxons because a group of them landed on Southampton Water and took Winchester, founding the kingdom of Wessex. While attempting to advance further west, they were defeated at Mount Badon, probably Badbury (though this is much debated) and their conquest held in check for some fifty years. Legend suggests that King Arthur was responsible for this success.

The Angles founded a kingdom in Northumbria, which was supreme for a time in the seventh century. But before this, St Augustine had been sent to Kent by Pope Gregory and had converted the king, building a church in Canterbury. A daughter of this king had gone north and married the king of Northumbria. In 664 a great meeting, called the Synod of Whitby, was held to decide between the Roman form of Christianity and the Celtic. Christianity had been brought to Scotland from Ireland by many missionaries, the greatest of whom was St Columba. The Roman was chosen, so the authority of the pope was recognised in England. Northumbria declined in the late seventh century and Mercia, the central kingdom, took its place as the leading kingdom under Offa, who built the dyke to protect his lands from the Welsh.

Towards the end of Mercian domination in the late eighth century, the Vikings began their attacks and we turn to Wessex. In 802 Egbert became king of Wessex, the first of this great family to be well known as a ruler. He defeated the Mercians and became overlord of Britain. He also defeated the Vikings, but after his death they sacked London and in the mid-ninth century began to settle in the Isle of Sheppey.

During the reign of the next three kings of Wessex, the Viking or Danish great army invaded with the intention of occupying the whole country, and in 871 forced Alfred, who had recently succeeded his brothers, to make peace. Seven years later the Danes, now under Guthrum, attacked Alfred and compelled him to take refuge on the Isle of Athelney in the Somerset marshes. Some seven weeks later he had managed to collect together an army and came out of his hiding place (where the story of the cakes is said to have taken place, though this has no historical foundation) and defeated Guthrum at Ethandune. Guthrum was forced to make peace and to live north of Watling Street in Mercia, and with the addition of Northumbria this became the Danelaw. This was the area north of Wessex, where the Danes ruled.

Alfred could now turn to reorganising his kingdom. He realised the need for a navy and built ships, which defeated the Danes at sea. He built forts along his border with the Danes and reorganised his army. He turned his attention to the churches and rebuilt many that had been destroyed in the wars and invited scholars to his court. Craftsmen came to instruct his people in stone building. He made himself into a scholar and translated books into Anglo-Saxon including the *Anglo-Saxon Chronicle*. When he died in 899, it was clear that his greatness lay in the fact that he had devoted his life to preserving his people and Christianity from Danish destruction.

Under his two immediate successors, Edward and Athelstan, the conquest of the island was continued until 937 when Athelstan defeated an army of the north. This victory left him as the most powerful ruler in Europe and marked the great age of Anglo-Saxon monarchy. This continued during several short reigns until Ethelred succeeded. During his reign the invasions of the Danes restarted. This reign was a series of disasters and the king was called 'the Unready', meaning 'ill-advised', because he wouldn't listen to his advisers. He attempted to buy off the Danes by offering them money, which was collected in the form of a tax, the

Danegeld. Large sums were paid over, but the Danes returned for more, and eventually the Danish king, Canute, was chosen as king of England. He ruled as an English king and sent his Danish fleet home. He lived in England, though he also ruled Denmark and Norway, and the land settled down again in peace.

So peaceful and prosperous was the country that Canute went to Rome on a pilgrimage, leaving the country in the hands of Earl Godwin. Canute's two sons who succeeded him were not so successful, and on their deaths the *Witan*, the English Council, recalled the old Saxon line in the person of Edward the Confessor. He had lived in Normandy for many years where he knew Duke William and was more Norman than English and influenced by the Norman court. He appointed a Norman as Archbishop of Canterbury and filled his court with Norman followers. Earl Godwin's influence increased when Edward married his daughter. During the reign William of Normandy was said to have been promised the throne as Edward was childless. Godwin was banished for a time, but recalled by the *Witan* and restored to his earldom. He then died suddenly and his son Harold became earl. Meanwhile the king was occupied with the building of Westminster Abbey and left the running of the government to Harold.

Edward the Confessor had no children, so when he died, early in January 1066, the *Witan* chose Harold Godwinsson as king. Some years before, Harold had been shipwrecked on the shores of Normandy, and when brought before the local duke, William, had promised not to stand in the way of the latter's claim to the English throne. Harold had sworn over some relics that William should succeed to the throne when Edward the Confessor died. This gave William the backing of the pope for his invasion of England. When William heard of the accession of Harold he sent an embassy to claim the throne, but it was rejected and Harold gave orders to defend the coast. Meanwhile William prepared to invade, as portrayed in the Bayeux Tapestry, and landed at Pevensey Bay in October.

Harold's brother, Tostig, had joined with Harold Hardrada, a famous king of Norway, and invaded the north of England. Harold Godwinsson marched his army to Northumbria and defeated and killed Tostig and Harold Hardrada at Stamford Bridge. It was while he was celebrating this victory that he heard that William had arrived. Harold hurried back and the scene was set for one of the most famous battles in British history, that of Hastings on 14 October 1066.

Harold posted his men on the brow of a hill behind a strong palisade or fence, and William found that he could not break through and withdrew. This broke the ranks of the Saxons and the Normans turned to face the attackers, whom they destroyed. Harold, surrounded by his bodyguard, the housecarls, was now outnumbered, but continued fighting until killed, together with his brothers Leofwine and Gyrth. The defeat was total as so many Saxons were killed with their king or were scattered over the surrounding countryside. William built an abbey on the site.

Harold's body is claimed to have been buried at Waltham Abbey, though this is doubted. William moved slowly after his victory – it is thought he may have been ill – but he took Dover, then marched in the direction of London, hoping the *Witan* would offer him the crown. He marched west of the capital, crossed the Thames at Wallingford and pitched camp at Berkhamstead.

The *Witan* chose Edgar the Atheling as king, but it soon became clear that William was in control. By his move to Berkhamstead he had cut off all communications between London and the north. While William was at Berkhamstead, Edwin, Morcar and the leading Saxon nobles left after the Battle of Hastings came to William and offered him the crown, which he accepted. The coronation took place in Westminster Abbey on 25 December 1066. This famous year had now become the year of three kings.

As William had several sons, the dynasty would be safe if he could secure the throne. Harold's family was living in Exeter, and there the first rebellion took place. William dealt with this quite easily, but found the great rising of 1068–1069 much harder to quash.

Edwin and Morcar, two of the Saxon nobles not present at Hastings, rebelled in the north. William captured York, bought off a Viking fleet which had come to the help of the rebels, and laid waste the land between the Humber and the Tees. Morcar escaped and made a camp with Hereward in the Fens on the east coast. William captured this camp after some of the most desperate fighting of his whole career. This completed the conquest of England, and from this he derives his title of 'Conqueror'.

The defeat at Hastings had meant that William was able to divide his enemies, who had no notable Saxon figure to unite behind. But the country had to remain conquered because of the small numbers of Normans in England, and so we turn to William's methods of retaining his land.

William used various ways to keep a hold on his newly conquered land. His highly disciplined and mobile army was able to divide his enemies and so he could build castles wherever suitable. These were usually of the motte and bailey type, though the shape of the landscape often made other styles more appropriate. These were built of wood first, for speed of conquest, and only when times became more peaceful did their holders rebuild them in stone. Settlements grew up round them for local defence, the origins of many of our towns. Notably the most famous example of this type of building to overawe a local population is the Tower of London, built on the east side of the city; but primarily they were places where a few soldiers could be based and used if necessary.

William inherited a system of landholding, this being the source of wealth. He developed this during the years of his reign, attempting to make the king the source of all land distribution. To see how effective this was, we need to look briefly at the Domesday Book. This was a survey which he ordered to be carried out towards the end of his reign, which was available to William's officials in 1086 and is still available to be studied. It can be described as a rent roll by which the king could know the strength of his resources.

The basic idea was that tenants held land from the king, paid rent in the form of military service and certain moneys, and in return expected to be protected. William usually took care to see that grants of land were scattered rather than in one block. Tenants would then have difficulty in concentrating their forces against the monarch, though a great deal would still depend on the personality of the king.

William was a very keen huntsman. He enclosed parts of Hampshire to make the New Forest and strict laws were enforced here. Two of his family were killed accidentally while hunting.

His attitude towards the Church was to be expected. As far as possible he kept it under his control, deposing the last archbishop of Canterbury, Stigand, because he had approved of Harold's coronation and appointing Lanfranc from the Abbey of Bec in his place. William, however, maintained the independence of the Church from Rome, always a popular move in England, and refused to do homage to the pope for his crown.

So William established his control over most of the country in varying degrees of strength – he was probably not so powerful in Cornwall, the north of England and Wales, but the population knew who was king and the *Anglo-Saxon Chronicle* speaks highly of his reign. Nevertheless, it should be mentioned that Norman influence in England had begun before Hastings was fought, and William was fortunate in that Harold had finally defeated the Vikings, so there was no threat from Scandinavia. He was also fortunate in that he had a strong base in Normandy and found so little resistance in England after 1066. He was a strong man physically and had a powerful personality. On his death in 1087, fighting in France, his eldest son, Robert, took the family possessions of Normandy; his second son, another William, came to England, and was crowned in Westminster Abbey on Sunday, 26 September. The youngest surviving son, Henry, inherited money which he was able to use later.

William II was usually known as Rufus. He too was a strong character, inheriting much of his father's personality. William II maintained order because it was to his advantage to do so, but there was bound to be trouble with his elder brother, Robert, who thought that he should have inherited England as well as Normandy.

The first crusade took place during this reign and Robert was persuaded to go on it. He needed money and so sold Normandy to his brother, thus the two countries were united again as under the Conqueror. William Rufus also extended the conquest to parts of Wales, mainly in the south, building some castles there.

Northern England was invaded by Malcolm, King of Scots, but William II was a good soldier and overawed Malcolm with a large show of force, compelling Malcolm to do homage for his crown.

William took possession of parts of Cumberland, fortifying Carlisle. William was certainly the equal of his father as a soldier, and was more successful in his control of his lands, but his relationship with the Church was not so happy.

Archbishop Lanfranc, whom William I had appointed, died and William Rufus, who cared little for the Church, kept the post vacant for some four years, holding the revenues for himself. The king fell ill and hurriedly appointed Anselm, again from the Abbey of Bec. The two men could not agree on the Church's position in the government of the country and Anselm returned to Rome for the remainder of the reign.

This reign, which came to an end with the king's accidental death while hunting in the New Forest, was an important one. William had continued the strong government policy of his father and avoided civil war, which might well have taken place if Robert had succeeded.

As William died in 1100 there had already been thirty-four years of comparative peace since Hastings, a long period at any time in British history. However, it should be remembered that the mass of Englishmen's lives would have been affected more by the attitude of the local lord than by a king in London. A powerful central monarchy would have been able to insist on peace locally, and we shall see later on what happened when this was not the case.

William's younger brother, Henry, was conveniently near when William was killed. He was to prove another capable ruler and he seized the throne immediately. From the terms of his father's will he was already a wealthy man and so there was comparative peace in the country. The Conqueror's youngest son, Henry I, was born after the Battle of Hastings, in 1070. As has been already mentioned, he was in England when William Rufus was killed. This has given rise to rumours of a palace *coup d'état*, but this seems unlikely on present evidence. Certainly he was near Winchester and immediately moved there to claim the Treasury. He recalled Archbishop Anselm and the king's coronation took place as soon as possible. He then married Matilda – a princess of Anglo-Saxon descent – and so when Robert invaded to claim the throne, the English nobility tended to support Henry. Robert withdrew with a pension to Normandy.

The king later invaded Normandy, now again under Robert's rule, and Robert was defeated at the Battle of Tinchebrai, considered by many as revenge for Hastings, so identified with the English had Henry become. Robert was blinded, possibly accidentally, and who would want a blind king? He was taken prisoner and spent the remainder of his long life in Gloucester Castle, dying in 1134 and being buried in the nearby cathedral.

Henry maintained the peace as his brother and father had done, but his relationship with the Church suffered. Anselm and the king quarrelled over who had the right to invest bishops with spiritual and temporal powers. The quarrel was settled for the time being by Henry retaining the temporal powers but granting the right of investing the ring and crozier on the newly consecrated bishops to the Church.

Henry's reign was a long one; it lasted for thirty-five years and was a firm and peaceful one. Thus there was a long section of prosperity of almost seventy years under these early Norman kings during which various forms of government that we recognise were becoming clearer.

The king's council ran the day-to-day business and settled any disputes between the lords of the land. The Great Council, which consisted of all tenants-in-chief, was summoned occasionally and the Court of the Exchequer managed the financial affairs of the country. This court was so called from the squared cloth which covered the table. There was no form of representative government of the whole people, such as we have now. That was a later development.

It should have become clear by now that the government of the country required a strong personality in order to run smoothly. The first three Norman kings were all very dominating, but Henry had no heir to succeed him. His son, Prince William, and a daughter, Mary, had been drowned in the disaster of the *White Ship* sunk off the Needles en route back to England from France after Mary's wedding in 1120. This left another daughter, Empress Matilda, as the heiress. Henry made the Great Council swear allegiance to her, which they did, but she was married to a foreigner, Geoffrey of Anjou, and was not well known at court. The country was not ready for rule by a woman, so on the king's death in France in 1135 from overeating, the Great Council went back on its oath of allegiance and Stephen, a nephew of Henry and cousin of Matilda, seized the throne, having reached England before his cousin had heard of her father's death. He had been one of the barons who had sworn to uphold Matilda's claim.

The next twenty years or so were to show what happened to a medieval country when there was no strong personality in charge. Stephen was popular with the English and a good soldier, but in a difficult position. In order to keep his supporters' loyalty, he had to let them do much as they pleased. This consisted of taking areas of land for themselves and building castles on land given them by the king in the form of bribes. Matilda was able to do this too and kept considerable support among those disaffected towards Stephen. Thus civil war came, but not nearly as savagely as has sometimes been suggested. The mass of the population did not side with one party or the other. Moreover, this was a period of great monastic activity. The abbeys of Tintern and Fountains were rising fast. The course of the reign was as follows.

Stephen was crowned, but Matilda immediately began her attempt to regain the throne. David of Scotland, Matilda's uncle, invaded the north, but was defeated at the Battle of the Standard at Northallerton. This strengthened Stephen's position considerably. In 1141 Stephen was defeated and taken prisoner at Lincoln, but Matilda had not endeared herself to her supporters by her overbearing attitude, and Stephen was exchanged for Robert of Gloucester – Matilda's illegitimate half-brother – and the war resumed. Matilda found the strain of war too much and withdrew to her home in France, and there was an uneasy peace for six years.

By now her son, Henry Plantagenet, was old enough to take up the claim to his grandfather's throne on behalf of his mother. Stephen was ageing, and Henry was soon successful enough to force the signing of a treaty between himself and Stephen. This took place at Wallingford on the Thames, and by its terms Henry was acknowledged as Stephen's successor. This happened in 1153 and was soon followed by Stephen's death in 1154 and his burial at Faversham. Henry succeeded peacefully as Henry II.

The Norman system of government had survived the war and was in place for Henry to revive and use in his own way.

Chapter II
THE PLANTAGENETS

Henry II inherited a country which needed to have order restored after the wars of the previous reign, and he was the right man for the task. He was himself very energetic, very strong physically, rather short and with a violent temper, but at the same time a very approachable man.

He began by insisting that soldiers hired by Stephen from abroad should be sent home. Also he gave orders that any castles built during the last reign should be destroyed and grants of land made by the late king should be recalled. He needed to be energetic because he had extensive lands to look after. From his mother, Matilda, he had inherited England, Normandy and Maine. From his father, Geoffrey of Anjou, he held Anjou and Touraine. Henry had married the divorced wife of Louis VII, Eleanor, and he held, as a result of this marriage, Poitou and all the provinces south of the Loire to the Pyrenees.

In fact he held more of France than England in area and he compelled Malcolm of Scotland to do homage for his country. This was the act of loyalty paid by a man to his lord in exchange for his lands. The eastern half of Ireland was subdued later in the reign, so that by 1171 Henry ruled from Dublin to the Spanish frontier. This was an immense area to cover and Henry was always on the move somewhere as most early kings had no fixed capital city.

Henry's relationship with the Church was not so successful. He wanted to reform church government and make everybody subject to the king's courts in legal matters. But the Church was a very powerful part of the community. Henry chose as archbishop in 1164 his great friend Becket. On being appointed, Becket altered his way of life completely from that of a rich and wealthy man and became a keen churchman, giving up his post as chancellor and now opposing Henry's ideas.

Becket did reluctantly agree to the Constitutions of Clarendon which said that all criminal cases should be tried in the royal courts, but shortly afterwards rejected them and appealed to the pope for support. Becket was summoned to appear before the king at a council held at Northampton but defied the king and fled to Louis VII.

Henry then proceeded to have his son, another Henry, crowned as co-king by the archbishop of York. Henry did not trust his barons when they promised to acknowledge his son as king after him. They had broken their promises to his mother, the Empress Matilda, but could not break a coronation oath. Louis VII and the pope compelled Becket and Henry to be reconciled and the archbishop returned to Canterbury.

On his return he excommunicated the archbishop of York and those bishops who had supported him at the coronation. When Henry heard about this he lost his temper, and four knights, encouraged by his words, sailed across the Channel and murdered Becket in Canterbury Cathedral on 29 December 1170. Henry was appalled by the murder and later did penance in the cathedral. Becket was made a saint by the pope in 1173.

While the problem of Becket was in progress, Henry continued with the reorganisation of the law and with the unwritten British constitution. He had already restored order after Stephen's reign and now he established the idea of trial by jury. The country was divided into six circuits and justices sent round to administer the law.

Henry wanted to limit the power of the nobility and intro-duced the idea of payment in money instead of military service. Thus the king could hire soldiers and was not so dependent on the services of his barons. This suited many of them also as they could now remain on their estates. Henry was thus able to have a national army.

Henry's large family was growing up, and his sons wanted lands of their own to administer. Henry did not want to split his kingdom up, but Eleanor, his wife, encouraged them to rebel against their father. The king of France, who was always anxious to harm the English, joined them against Henry but the latter was very powerful and in 1174 crushed the rebellion. At the same time the Scottish king, William the Lion, invaded northern England, but was defeated and captured at Alnwick. He was made to do homage for Scotland before being released.

Prince Henry and Prince Geoffrey rebelled again in 1183, but Prince Henry died suddenly of a fever and Geoffrey was killed in a tournament. This left Richard and John to make trouble. Some years later, Richard, assisted by the new king of France, Philip, expelled Henry from Touraine. Henry was now an old man and no longer the strong king of his youth. His death came in 1189 and was partly due to disappointment when he found that John too had joined the rebels at the suggestion of his mother whom Henry had imprisoned. So ended a long and very successful reign. Henry was buried at Fontevraud with other members of his family, leaving the throne to his son Richard, the crusader king.

There was no opposition to Richard's accession, one sign of his father's success. Richard immediately began his plans for crusading. For this he needed money. The crown revenues were not enough so he sold charters to towns, government posts in Church and state and land belonging to both. Many towns date their charters from this period.

The crusades were the military expeditions which the Christian powers undertook to try to capture Palestine from the Muslims.

The king then left for the Holy Land. He stopped at Cyprus, where he married Berengaria of Navarre, who never came to England. There he joined up with Philip of France and went on to relieve Acre. The crusaders moved south, hugging the coast, and won a battle at Arsouf, but much to Richard's disappointment they were unable to capture Jerusalem. Richard and Philip had quarrelled after Acre and Philip had returned to France to try to regain some of his territory which Richard controlled. Disunion crept in amongst the crusading leaders and Richard and Leopold of Austria fell out. A peace was concluded with the Saracen leader, Saladin, and Richard set off for England. He sailed up the Adriatic and attempted to cross overland through Germany. He was captured by Leopold and handed over to the emperor. Later he was freed on payment of a ransom equivalent to twice the annual crown revenues and returned to England, where he stayed for about six months.

Richard then went to France to try to settle matters with Philip. While doing so he heard of a discovery of possible treasure at the castle of Chaluz. He besieged the castle and was wounded in the shoulder. The wound was not attended to properly and he died in 1199, forgiving the soldier who had wounded him.

He was in England for very little of his reign, yet his father's legal and constitutional arrangements functioned well and Richard remained extremely popular in his absence. He was taken and buried at Fontevraud. His wife, Berengaria, died many years later, in about 1230 at the convent of L'Espan. There were no children and Henry II's youngest son, John, claimed the throne and succeeded.

In history generally John has a poor reputation because of the problems he faced and was not able to deal with. There were three problems in particular which covered his entire reign.

Firstly John had to deal with his nephew. John's elder brother, Geoffrey, had left a son named Arthur, and a claim to the throne was made on his behalf. Legally this was a good claim, but Arthur was in Brittany and was only fourteen years old, so the barons accepted John's claim as the man on the spot and he was crowned. Philip of France joined with Arthur, but Arthur was captured trying to take the castle of Mirabeau, where his grandmother was staying. Arthur was taken to Rouen and murdered there. Philip then summoned John to pay homage for the lands he owned in France and John refused. Philip advanced into King John's French lands and took over all of them except the Channel Islands, La Rochelle and Poitou.

The second problem facing John concerned the appointment of a new archbishop of Canterbury. Archbishop Hubert had died and the younger monks of Canterbury elected their sub-prior to take his place. The older ones were instructed by the king to choose the bishop of Norwich, John de Grey. Both sides appealed to Pope Innocent III, who set aside both elections and sent Stephen Langton, who was an Englishman. John refused to accept the appointment and the pope excommunicated all England and put the people under a papal interdict, which meant most services in churches were forbidden. John still refused to yield and the pope excommunicated the king. John retaliated by seizing church property. The pope then declared John deposed and called on Philip to invade to enforce the order. John submitted to the pope, which meant that the pope had to call on Philip to stop his invasion as John was now a papal subject. Philip was furious and attacked John's ally, the count of Flanders. John asked the emperor for help, but their combined armies were defeated at Bouvines. This was one of the most important battles of the century as it confirmed the loss of English possessions in Normandy and other parts of France and weakened John.

For his continental wars John had taxed all classes heavily and his attitude towards the baronial class was one of insolence and tyranny. He had lost their continental possessions and so they met at St Albans under the leadership of Stephen Langton and Robert Fitz-Walter where a declaration of grievances was made. At St Paul's in London, Stephen Langton then produced the coronation charter of Henry I and this was accepted by the barons as the basis of their demands. They then moved to Bury St Edmunds and took an oath that they would compel the king to seal a charter of freedom.

John asked for three months to consider this and used the time to try to split the unity of the opposition. He also took the oath of a crusader to put himself under the protection of the Church.

The barons again assembled and marched to London where they were very well received. This support from the city made them decide on their course of action and they marched to Windsor to meet the king. Meanwhile, John's support seems to have rapidly declined, and the barons were able to compel him to seal the charter at Runnymede on the Thames in 1215.

The Great Charter, or Magna Carta, had sixty-three clauses. Amongst the most important were the ones that stated that justice should not be sold or delayed to anyone, that tenants should be taxed according to rank, that the Church should continue to possess its rights, that London and other cities should retain their privileges and that foreign traders should be encouraged. It was an early attempt to show the difference between the duties of a king

25

and the rights of the people.

The pope disallowed the charter and John hired mercenary troops and began to ravage the north in the Lincoln area. The barons invited the French *Dauphin*, Louis, to come over and he was well received in London. John continued what has been described as a brilliant campaign in the north-east, but while crossing the Wash lost his baggage and the crown jewels. He retired to Swineshead Abbey near Newark, a sick man, and died there soon after. He was taken across England to Worcester and buried in the cathedral, a foundation which he had always much liked.

The situation for the monarchy at John's death was difficult. John had married twice and his successor was from the second marriage and was only nine. The barons had recently compelled the king to sign the charter and the pope had annulled it. The barons had then asked Louis to succeed to the throne. Henry III, the young son of John, was very fortunate in his regents. The earl of Pembroke and Hubert de Burgh had the young king crowned as soon as possible at Gloucester and many of the barons rallied to Henry III. Louis was defeated at Lincoln by Pembroke and Hubert destroyed a fleet bringing help from France. Louis signed a treaty with Pembroke and returned to France.

Unfortunately the young king, in what was to be the third longest reign in our history so far, grew up to be an indefinite type of man, much inclined to give court appointments to his wife's relations and to his half-brothers, for his mother had remarried after John's death. One of the uncles of his wife, Queen Eleanor, became archbishop of Canterbury and the government passed into the hands of people who had little knowledge of the English.

Henry was then persuaded to invade France to try to regain the lands lost by his father, but was defeated and lost Poitou. He returned and spent a considerable part of his time and money in the rebuilding of the east end of Westminster Abbey. The nave was finished later, financed largely by a famous lord mayor, Dick Whittington.

All these problems that Henry III faced gave the barons another chance to rebel and try to correct some of their grievances. These troubles were really a continuation of those under John. The king's brother-in-law led the barons: his name was Simon de Montfort.

They presented the king and his son Edward with a proposal that they should accept permanent advisers and a committee to manage financial affairs. The king refused and civil war broke out. Henry and his brother were taken prisoner at the Battle of Lewes and a treaty made whereby Prince Edward gave himself up as a ransom for his father. Simon de Montfort was now master of the country and summoned his famous Parliament of 1265, the first House of Commons. It represented all classes of the country, including as it did barons, clergy and two knights from each county and, for the first time, representatives from the chief towns and boroughs. Unfortunately, Simon was not supported by the whole country and a reaction set in in favour of the king, largely because of jealousy among the barons of Simon's position. Prince Edward escaped from captivity, raised an army and defeated and killed Simon at Evesham. Henry was restored to full authority, provided he accepted the charter.

The king was now an old man and the real government was in the hands of Prince Edward. The country settled down very quickly after the civil war and by 1270 was so peaceful that Edward was able to join the ninth crusade and was abroad when his father died in 1272.

Chapter III

FIGHT FOR THE CROWN

Even though Edward I was away on a crusade when Henry III died, the accession was assured. He did not reach England until two years later when he was crowned in the presence of his nobility and Alexander III, king of Scots, at Westminster.

As heir to the throne Edward had had a chance to be involved in the running of the kingdom and came to the throne with a high military reputation and with some experience of how the law worked. He realised too that England, Scotland and Wales would function much better as a single unit, rather than as three separate states, and so a large proportion of his reign consisted of attempts to unify the country, successful in Wales but not in Scotland.

Three years after his return Edward invaded Wales where he first saw how effective the longbow would be. This country was geographically more open to invasion than the north. Prince Llewellyn was forced to retire to the hills of Snowdon. War had broken out because Llewellyn's bride, the daughter of Simon de Montfort, had been detained in England as a hostage to her future husband's loyalty and refused permission to join him. As Llewellyn was confined to Anglesey and Snowdon, his brother David took arms in central Wales. The two brothers attempted to join up, but Llewellyn was killed in a skirmish at Builth-on-Wye. Shortly after, David was captured and executed at Shrewsbury.

This seems to have ended serious Welsh resistance and Edward took over the government of Wales, giving his newly-born son, later Edward II, to the Welsh as their prince. Wales was governed from Ludlow and not represented in the English Parliament until the reign of Henry VIII.

In order to impress the Welsh and ensure peace in the north of the principality, Edward started the building of his famous castles in that part. He ordered castles to be built at Beaumaris, Caernarvon and Conwy. We notice how castles had developed from Norman times and also the crusader influence that Edward introduced with the assistance of his architect.

Edward's problems with Scotland were very different from those he had faced so successfully in Wales. Much longer distances were involved for a medieval army. But it is probably true to say that none of these difficulties need have arisen if Edward's original plan had succeeded. He offered his son in marriage to Margaret of Scotland. She was living in Norway and on her accession at the death of Alexander III set sail for Scotland but fell ill and died of pneumonia after being shipwrecked on Orkney. Moreover, parts of Wales had already been settled by Norman invaders before Edward attacked, but this was not so in Scotland, where a separate state under a long line of kings had existed for many years. Though there had been encounters with the Scots on the borders before, they remained fiercely independent.

Eventually three claimants to the throne came forward and Edward was asked to decide upon one of them. At Norham, near Berwick, he gave a just and legal decision in favour of John Balliol, who accepted the throne and was crowned at Scone. Edward became involved in war with France and ordered Balliol to supply troops. The order was ignored and Balliol invaded England. Edward returned from France and marched against Balliol, whom he defeated at Dunbar. Balliol was sent to England, later being exiled to France. Scotland was put under military rule, which the Scots did not accept.

On Edward's withdrawal, thinking that there no longer existed a Scottish problem, a Lowland knight, William Wallace by name, gathered an army and defeated the English at Stirling Bridge and invaded England. He burnt and destroyed property in the Newcastle area. Edward advanced once more and met Wallace near Falkirk, where he defeated him. Wallace continued to resist for some years until he was betrayed in 1305, taken to London and executed. It is important to note two things: the Stone of Scone, on which Scottish kings were enthroned, had been taken to Westminster Abbey where it was kept on show until its recent return to Scotland, and the Battle of Falkirk was won by the longbow men.

The struggle for independence continued under Balliol's nephew, John Comyn, another claimant to the Scottish throne, who defeated the English at Roslin, south of Edinburgh. Edward invaded again and signed a treaty with Comyn which placed the government in Edward's hands; on his withdrawal Comyn was murdered in church at Dumfries by Robert Bruce, grandson of one of the original claimants to the throne. Edward was nearly seventy and set out once more to invade Scotland, but died at Burgh-by-Sands, leaving the task to his son, Edward II.

Edward II was not so interested in uniting the various parts of Britain as his father, and withdrew to London. Bruce continued the war capturing castle after castle, but Stirling held out against him. However, the governor, facing starvation in the castle, agreed to hand over the castle if help had not arrived by 24 June 1314. Edward II marched north with what was an enormous army for the period, but was defeated at Bannockburn with great losses and only escaped himself with some difficulty. Scotland regained its independence and kept it until a Scottish king, James VI, became James I of England.

Edward I's reputation as a great king is not only founded on his military capacity, but also on his ability to govern. In this respect various reforms were instituted. The law courts were reorganised into the Court of the King's Bench, the Court of the Common Pleas and the Court of the Exchequer. The first complete Parliament was summoned in 1295, which included the three groups of Lords, Commons and clergy.

Various far-reaching laws were passed. These included one to establish the rights of the people to landed property and so defined what taxes they owed the crown. Also there was an act to establish the succession of heirs to estates. An act was passed encouraging each class of person to provide themselves with arms for the defence of the country and that officers should be appointed (Justices of the Peace) to ensure that gates of towns should be shut at sunset and that each area should be responsible for crimes committed in it. Parliament also passed an act when Edward was away in Ghent that the king should not obtain taxes without the agreement of the people. Edward signed this one in Ghent.

Problems with Parliament were still continuing when Edward died.

Edward's first wife died in 1290. She was Eleanor of Castile and the king was devastated by her death which took place at Grantham. The king raised crosses where the coffin rested on its way to Westminster for burial. There were twelve of these of which three, those at Waltham, Northampton and Geddington, remain. The most famous was the last one on the journey at Charing Cross – the name comes from the French *chère reine* meaning 'beloved queen' – but it no longer exists. Edward later married Margaret of France who survived the king.

Apart from the Scottish campaign which ended in his enormous defeat, Edward II, who succeeded in 1307, was concerned more with home affairs. He was a very different character from his father and in his youth had been rather over-looked by him. He had been expected to be a soldier but seemed more interested in thatching, swimming and gardens and avoided public business whenever possible. This indolence was to be brought up at the time of his deposition. He was too much under the influence of favourites, but he was king for twenty years.

His first favourite, Piers Gaveston, was a French knight, who had been banished by the late king and whom Edward I had asked his son not to bring back when he lay dying at Burgh-by-Sands. As soon as the old king died, Piers was recalled and made earl of Cornwall.

Edward's cousin, Thomas, earl of Lancaster, led the barons in a demand for Gaveston's removal and Edward sent him to Ireland as lord deputy. The barons in Parliament then tried to regulate the king's household and reform his methods of governing inherited from Edward I. The series of rules which they drew up would have curtailed the king's activities considerably so the king recalled Piers. Unfortunately for the king, Piers was captured and executed by the earl of Warwick.

Edward now took as his favourites the Despensers, father and son, but the barons were disgusted at this further example of royal misrule and joined Lancaster in revolt. They were defeated at Boroughbridge, north-west of York, and Lancaster was executed at Pontefract.

Meanwhile Edward's wife, Isabella, had parted from him and gone to France. She invaded, assisted by her lover, Roger Mortimer, landed in Suffolk and assumed royal powers. They captured and hanged the Despensers. Parliament was called and deposed Edward on the grounds of incompetence, the loss of Scotland at Bannockburn, his refusal to listen to the advice of his barons, and the breaking of his coronation oath. The king agreed to these points and his son succeeded him as Edward III. In medieval times, to be a deposed king was tantamount to being a dead one, and shortly afterwards Edward was murdered in Berkeley Castle and buried in Gloucester Cathedral. It would seem to have been a reign with little to commend it, but it did see the beginning of the idea that no order was valid in law unless the Commons had agreed to it.

Edward III succeeded when he was fourteen and did not take over the government for a year or two, leaving it to his mother and Mortimer. However, within three years he assumed royal power with the backing of the nobility. He seized Nottingham Castle and had Mortimer arrested, tried and executed for his part in the deposition of his father. Queen Isabella, his mother, was confined in comfortable imprisonment in Castle Rising in Norfolk for the rest of her long life, where the king often used to visit her.

The new king, who was to reign for just on fifty years, had military talent which he wanted to use. He first attacked and defeated the Scots at Halidon Hill and placed Edward Balliol, son of John, on the throne; but this move did not succeed and Edward Balliol fled from Scotland, David II being re-established.

Meanwhile Edward had turned his attention to France and what has become known as the Hundred Years War had begun. Before describing some of the battles of the first part of the war, it would be useful to know the reasons for the war.

Edward wanted to take revenge on the French for helping the Scots in their resistance to England over the past years. Philip of France had invaded Gascony, the area of France where a great deal of the English wine trade took place; but perhaps most important of all for England's economy, Philip was interfering in England's wool trade. This was the point which gained Edward most support from Parliament and the people. Wine and wool were then the main reasons for the war. After the war began, Edward claimed the French throne through right of descent from his mother. It was a very weak claim but French lilies remained on the English royal arms until 1801.

The first campaign was not a great success. Edward invaded north-east France, but could not bring the French to battle, though he did win a great naval battle off Sluys in 1340. Six years later he invaded again, this time in company with his sixteen-year-old son, the Black Prince, as he became known. The king advanced to near Paris but again could not persuade the French to fight so retreated to Calais and found the French at a little village called Crécy. Here he defeated them with much loss of life, and then besieged Calais. This siege took eleven months, a delay which made the king very angry. He was about to take revenge on some leading citizens of the city when his wife, Philippa, intervened on their behalf and begged forgiveness for them, which the king gave. The queen took them away and had them looked after before release. Calais became a very important and wealthy port, enjoying great prosperity.

Ten years later the Black Prince led his own expedition from Bordeaux where he was living. He marched northwards, destroying the countryside, and met the French king near Poitiers. Here he totally defeated the French and captured John, their king. This battle, and a few succeeding campaigns by the Black Prince, led to peace being signed at Brétigny. By this treaty Edward retained his conquests, but gave up the claim to the French throne and John was to be released from the Tower on payment of an enormous ransom. He returned to France to collect the money, but was unable to raise the whole amount and so returned to England, dying a prisoner in the Savoy Palace.

War broke out again in 1369, but went badly for England. The Black Prince was not well and the king was ageing, and by 1374 all had been lost except for Bordeaux, Bayonne and Calais. The Black Prince returned to England and died in 1376 before his father.

The gap in the French campaigns between Crécy and Poitiers was partly caused by the most famous outbreak of the Black Death, a form of bubonic plague which travelled across Europe at this time and continued to break out sporadically until the final savage attack in 1665. It reached England in 1349 from the East, carried by fleas on rats in ships' holds, and as far as we can tell from the records killed about half the population. There was naturally a shortage of farm workers and other labourers in England, and Parliament passed an act fixing wages at the rate they were before the outbreak.

Other acts passed during this long reign concerned the checking of papal influence and the passing by Parliament of the Treason Act. This was an important act for it said, among other things, that it was treason to kill the king or his eldest son, to attack the king, to help the king's enemies, to forge coins or to kill the chancellor, treasurer or justices. Also, Parliament began to take more control of the financial affairs of the country by saying that no tax should be put on wool without its consent.

This long reign, probably better known for its military exploits, was particularly important in establishing that parliamentary consent was required for raising money, that the Lords and Commons must agree on alterations in the laws, and also that Parliament had powers of impeachment. This latter measure meant that the Commons could try someone before the Lords, who would act as judges.

The fiftieth anniversary of Edward's accession was not celebrated, because by then the king had become senile and was very much under the influence of a favourite, Alice Perrers, the first person to be impeached. This took place after the old king's death. Edward's wife, Philippa, had died in 1369, and the old king himself died in 1377 at Westminster, with Alice in attendance, leaving the throne to a minor, the Black Prince's son, Richard.

Once again England had a boy as king. Richard was eleven on succeeding. He was very popular as the son of the Black Prince and because of his good looks and youth. This was particularly fortunate as his uncle, John of Gaunt, and his other uncles were very unpopular at this time through their misconduct of the war, and they were to find it very useful to have the boy to hide their unpopularity behind. Richard does not seem to have had an official regent. On state occasions his mother, Joan of Kent, acted with him, but Richard had his own seal. The actual government was carried on by a council of twelve ministers.

In 1381 the Peasants' Revolt took place. The immediate cause of the revolt was the imposition of a poll tax on every adult person. John Ball, a priest of Kent, had been going round preaching ideas of liberty and equality for some twenty years, and there were also economic reasons for the sudden uprising resulting from the Black Death. This disease continued to break out, though not as fiercely as it had in 1349. The poll tax was imposed to help pay for the French wars which were now no longer so popular as they were not showing much success.

The revolt extended over the east and south-east counties. In Essex, Jack Straw was the leader; in Kent, Wat Tyler. The rebels marched on London, burning documents as they went and putting to death lawyers and judges. They hoped to talk to the king and have their grievances attended to by him. They demanded the abolition of villeinage – which was unpaid service on the lord's land while living rent-free – reduction of rents, free access to markets and a general pardon when they met Richard and his council at Mile End. The demands were granted and they dispersed. Meanwhile the Kentish rebels attacked the Tower of London and murdered the archbishop and lord chancellor. There were riots in London and John of Gaunt's palace was burnt down. Richard agreed to meet them at Smithfield, thus drawing them away from central London. Wat Tyler was killed here by the lord mayor, who thought Tyler was going to strike the king, and for a few minutes the situation looked very dangerous. Richard, now fifteen, showed his character and took charge, promising charters of freedom, and the rebels went home quietly. Though now of age, the king was unable to resist the demands of his council to punish the rebels and he watched as sentence of death was passed on many as he and a large army marched through Kent and Essex. But we should note that landowners were not so enthusiastic about enforcing the demands of villeinage on their estates after the rebellion, and it gradually died out as a system.

Richard had no personal political party behind him at this stage of his reign and tended to favour the de Vere family; so in 1386 a council was appointed to take over the government. The king now began to build up a following, but in 1388 some of his council impeached and executed several of his friends, including his tutor Simon Burley and de Vere. Richard never forgot what had happened, but he waited until he was strong enough politically to take action. A year later he suddenly acted by dismissing his guardians and assumed sole authority with the agreement of Parliament and, it would appear, the people. He proved himself a capable ruler and ruled well for the next eight years, giving the country some of the best government of the Middle Ages.

By 1397 he was at the height of his powers and was beginning to act as though he was an absolute monarch in sole charge. This idea had been fought against in previous reigns. His court was almost oriental in the way he expected people to honour him. The situation does seem to have been accepted by Parliament because the king was granted customs duties for life, making him financially independent. His much-beloved first wife, Anne of Bohemia, had died in 1394 and this loss meant that he had nobody to restrain him.

A quarrel broke out between his cousin, Henry of Lancaster, and Thomas Mowbray, Duke of Norfolk. Parliament agreed to single combat between them, but the king settled the matter himself by banishing Lancaster for ten years and Norfolk for life. The king promised that if Henry's father, John of Gaunt, died while he was in exile, his estates would still come to him. In 1399 John died and Richard immediately confiscated all his estates. Henry of Lancaster returned and came ashore at Ravenspur in Lancashire, saying that he had come to claim his father's estates, but was received with such enthusiasm that he put forward a claim to the throne.

Meanwhile Richard had taken a second expedition to Ireland, but, hearing of Henry's landing, sailed back, expecting Henry's submission. Instead he found his own support rapidly declining and surrendered to Henry. He was imprisoned and compelled to resign his crown on the grounds of misgovernment and tyranny. Henry was declared king and Richard imprisoned in Pontefract Castle. Within a year he had died mysteriously, and his body lay in state in St Paul's before being buried at King's Langley. What he attempted to do, namely to crush the power of the nobles and avoid expensive wars, was what later kings such as Edward IV and Henry VII were able to do when the nobility had lost much of its strength after the Wars of the Roses and the nation was anxious for peace under strong government.

Henry IV's claim to the throne was weak, and so the reign was a disturbed one. Richard had relatives who rebelled on his behalf, but the easy suppression of this first rebellion did not stop others from attempting to remove Henry.

The Percy family of Northumberland claimed that Henry owed them for their help in putting him on the throne, and allied themselves with Owen Glendower. Henry had already made several attempts to subdue Glendower, the Welsh prince, who had been brought up as a squire at Richard's court. The earl of Northumberland's son, Harry Hotspur, advanced towards Shrewsbury to join up with Glendower's troops, but was met by Henry outside the town and defeated and slain. Northumberland was pardoned and fined. Some months later Northumberland and Archbishop Scrope of York raised a rebellion, but Scrope was captured and executed. Three years later Northumberland tried again, but was defeated and slain near Tadcaster at Bramham Moor.

Henry showed himself a very capable soldier both before and during his reign, and was able to pass the throne on to his son in 1413, but his position was always an uneasy one, and during his reign the House of Commons obtained the exclusive right to give grants of money to the monarch. Power was beginning to move from the king to the elected representatives.

Henry had campaigned abroad before becoming king but suffered from epilepsy from which he was to die. He had always wanted to lead a crusade to Jerusalem. When he fell ill for the last time, he was taken to the Jerusalem Chamber in Westminster Palace and there he died.

His son, another Henry, succeeded as Henry V, but to a very insecure hold on the throne. He realised this, and one of his first acts was to have the body of his cousin, Richard II, removed from King's Langley and re-interred in Westminster Abbey, to prove Richard was really dead.

A conspiracy against Henry was formed in favour of the earl of March, the rightful heir according to some. Henry put this down with considerable ferocity, ordering the execution of the chief conspirators.

The new king wanted to take his nobles' minds off the problem of the succession and so revived the idea of attacking France. This was not always popular with the Lords and Commons, who would have to provide the money for it. So Henry resumed the claim to the French throne originally made by his great-grandfather Edward III and invaded France at Harfleur with thirty thousand men.

Harfleur surrendered after a dreadful siege of several weeks, but the English army lost almost half its original numbers and Henry decided to return to England via Calais. On his way there he found the road barred by a large French army – often numbered at around twenty thousand – under the constable of France. Henry relied on his archers and the French on massed cavalry charges. Henry's army was in a poor state after the siege of Harfleur, but the French were determined to fight.

Henry drew up his forces between two woods, near a village called Agincourt. At about 11 a.m. he gave the order to advance. It had been raining and was very wet. The English archers built a palisade in front of them to defend themselves. The French cavalry charged the English line, but floundered in the mud and took fright at the swarm of arrows which hit them. Behind them the French men-at-arms tried to force their way forward, but found they could hardly handle their weapons. The English archers used their longbows to great effect. In places there were corpses piled up head high. Prisoners were taken, but later orders were given for no prisoners to be taken and some were killed. Losses are difficult to compute. The French dead are usually put at about seven thousand, of whom approximately seventeen hundred were knights. The English losses – up to seven hundred – included one knight, the Duke of York, who was smothered under a press of bodies in the mud.

Henry went home after this extraordinary defeat of the French, but returned two years later and captured many towns in Normandy. The king was proving himself to be a first-class general, and when the Burgundians joined him, he was able to bring about the Treaty of Troyes. This stated that Henry should marry the French king's daughter, Catherine, and succeed to the French throne after the French king's death.

The war continued, and Henry, after another brief visit to

England with his queen, returned to France and was campaigning near Vincennes when he fell ill and died.

His son, Henry VI, was eight months old when his father died and so required a protector and a regent in France. Henry V's brother, the Duke of Bedford, took these titles, and during his absences in France the Duke of Gloucester, another brother, acted for him in England. The English continued to secure victories and by 1428 they were ready to besiege Orleans, the entry to the south of France.

At this point in the war, when French morale was at its lowest point, something quite unique happened. The French king, Charles VII, was persuaded to allow a French peasant girl, Joan from Domrémy in Arc, to take five thousand troops to relieve Orleans. This she did, rallying the French with great enthusiasm. She then continued her victorious advance, winning a very important battle at Patay, where she defeated the earl of Shrewsbury, considered the best general of the period after Henry V.

Joan then led Charles VII to Reims for his coronation. Joan had now completed the task that the voices of an early vision had told her to do and asked to be allowed to go home, but she was too valuable to the king and his generals. Things now began to go wrong for her and she was captured by the Burgundians at Compiègne and handed over to the English who burnt her as a witch at Rouen in 1431. Charles made no attempt to save her, but a gradual loss of all France now took place for the English and by 1453 only Calais was left in English hands.

Meanwhile the king, Henry VI, had grown up into a character difficult to describe. He was highly educated and intelligent and very interested in schools. He founded Eton and King's College, Cambridge. He was generous to the poor and his devotional life was well known, and yet this long reign of nearly forty years seems a series of disasters.

Henry had married Margaret of Anjou in 1445, but for many years there was no son and his cousin, Richard, Duke of York, remained as heir. Henry seems to have inherited from his French grandfather some mental instability, and in 1454 entered a period when he was unable to recognise anybody or take any part in the government. The Duke of York was made protector, but was displaced by the Duke of Somerset – a favourite of the queen's. The Duke of York, as heir apparent, took up arms against the king and a period of civil war began which is often called the Wars of the Roses. Many battles were fought, especially after the birth of a prince of Wales, and in 1460 Henry was defeated at Northampton and taken prisoner. Richard, Duke of York, was proclaimed by the council as heir presumptive to Henry. The next year the queen defeated Richard at Wakefield and had him executed. Richard's son, Edward, a much better general than his father, defeated Queen Margaret and the earl of Somerset at Towton in a snow-storm. Edward was now crowned as Edward IV and Henry and Margaret fled to Scotland.

The new king was a popular nineteen-year-old. For his time he was very tall, being over six foot. He had already proved himself as a general, and when the wars continued he again defeated the Lancastrians, as Henry VI's side was now being called. Edward led the Yorkists. Edward had married Elizabeth Woodville, a widow five years older than the king with a fifteen-year-old son. The marriage was a happy one and popular in London, but not at court, where many were jealous of her and her relations. Trouble was to come later in the reign because of this.

When Edward became king it was very necessary to restore some kind of law and order in the country and to reorganise the finances. He managed to do both and was the first English king for some time to be solvent.

Many other things concerned him, trade in particular. It was largely due to his private trading that he became so popular with the London merchants and was able to rebuild the family fortunes. Kings of England were still expected to live off their own estates. Also Edward kept England out of European wars, except on one occasion when, by a large display of force in France, he managed to make the French king, Louis XI, pay him to go back to England. Edward realised what few people had understood: England was not capable of conquering and holding France.

Meanwhile the earl of Warwick, who had not approved of the royal marriage, was reconciled with Queen Margaret, who had fled to France. Medieval English kings, as should be clear by now, depended on the support of their nobles, and this latest rebellion was a formidable one. Warwick, aided by Edward's brother Clarence, almost captured the king, who fled to Flanders. Henry VI was brought home to London and restored to the throne.

Edward was at Bruges preparing an army of invasion. He then copied the example of Henry IV and landed at Ravenspur, saying that he came to claim his duchy of York, not the throne. Few seem to have believed him, and as he marched south his army increased so much that he reclaimed the throne. Edward made straight for London, where Henry was living, and was recrowned. During his absence his elder son had been born. Edward then marched out of London and defeated Warwick at Barnet. Warwick was killed. Queen Margaret landed in the west and was defeated at Tewkesbury, where her son was killed. Some three weeks later Henry VI died, probably murdered.

The remainder of the reign was unremarkable. Edward patronised William Caxton, the printer, and competed with Henry in building by starting St George's Chapel, Windsor (where both kings are buried). When Edward died in 1483 he left a prosperous country, but once again the heir, his son Edward V, was under-age.

The late king's brother, Richard, Duke of Gloucester, met the young king on his way to London and escorted him the rest of the way. Richard was supported by Edward IV's council and was made protector for his nephew. The queen took refuge in Westminster Abbey with her younger son, another Richard, but was persuaded to give him up. Both boys were put in the Tower of London, which was then a royal residence. For some months they were seen playing together, but Richard then declared that Elizabeth Woodville was not Edward IV's lawful wife. Therefore the two young princes had no claim to the throne. Parliament offered the crown to Richard, who was crowned on the day originally chosen for his nephew's coronation.

Richard and his wife, Anne, went on a successful royal progress through England, but the princes disappeared. Tradition says they were murdered on the orders of their uncle, but this cannot be proved. Richard III faced a rebellion in 1483 from the Duke of Buckingham, but Richard captured him and he was executed at Salisbury.

Meanwhile the Lancastrians, in exile in France, were planning an invasion under Henry, earl of Richmond, grandson of Henry V's widow, Catherine, by her second marriage to Owen Tudor. Henry had a claim to the throne based on descent from Edward III's son, John of Gaunt. Henry set sail from Harfleur and landed at Milford Haven. He marched east and met Richard at Bosworth Field. There was fought a decisive battle. Richard had the larger army, but was deserted by Lord Stanley during the battle, leaving Henry victorious. Richard charged Henry, but was killed fighting bravely, and the gold circlet which had been round his helmet was placed on Henry's head on the battlefield. So we come to the end of the Wars of the Roses. They were a fight for the crown between the two rival houses of Lancaster and York. They were mainly wars between nobles, and the vast majority of the population took no part, but they did see the end of many noble families, thus increasing the power of the king. It is interesting to note how in these troubled times education and architecture flourished.

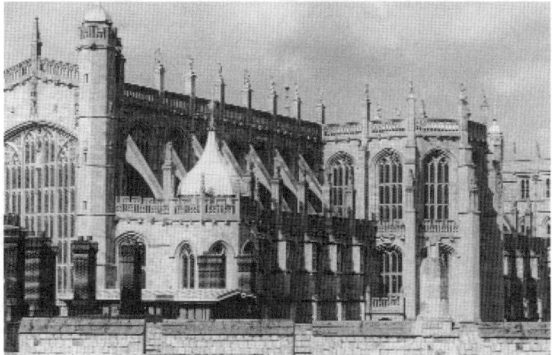

Top: Stonehenge.
Middle: Hampton Court Palace, main entrance.
Bottom: St George's Chapel, Windsor Castle.

Top: Ben Nevis. *Middle left:* Round Tower, Windsor Castle.
Middle right: Saxon coronation stone, Kingston upon Thames.
Bottom left: Boudicca in her chariot. *Bottom right:* Robert the Bruce.

Chapter IV
THE TUDOR DYNASTY

The year was 1485 and the period we have reached is known as Tudor. To those living at this time the Battle of Bosworth and the coronation of Henry VII must have seemed just events in the long series of wars. Few would have been able to remember a time when the nobles were not fighting amongst themselves. This is nevertheless an important date in British history, for it was to be the beginning of a new age.

Henry had first to establish himself as king. His predecessors Edward IV and Richard III had reinvigorated the machinery of government. One of the new king's first acts was to announce that he intended to marry Edward IV's daughter, Elizabeth, sister of the two princes who had recently disappeared in the Tower of London. He thereby united the two warring houses of Lancaster and York, but he showed that he disliked Yorkists and three attempts were made to remove the king. The first need not detain us. In the second a certain Lambert Simnel called himself the earl of Warwick (nephew of Richard III). To expose him the king paraded the real earl through London's streets. Simnel appeared in Dublin and was crowned there. He then landed in Lancashire but was defeated at Stoke and sent to work in the king's kitchens.

The third rebellion was a rather more dangerous matter. Perkin Warbeck from Tournai claimed to be the younger of the princes in the Tower. Many believed him for he had been well coached in his part and the French king acknowledged him. The Scottish king received him and Warbeck sailed for Cornwall. He failed to take Exeter in his advance towards London and fled to Beaulieu Abbey where he was captured, taken to London and later executed.

All was fairly quiet at home now, so Henry began to look for marriage alliances for his children. This would secure peace abroad and finally establish him as king. His elder son, Prince Arthur, married a Spanish princess, Catherine of Aragon, but died soon after. The two families did not want to lose the benefits of the alliance and so Catherine was engaged to the second son, Prince Henry.

Henry VII's elder daughter was married to the Scottish king, James IV, and so became the ancestress of the Stuart line, and the younger daughter, Mary, was married later to the elderly French king, Louis XI.

Henry VII governed through the Court of the Star Chamber with the consent of the two Houses of Parliament. The Star Chamber was necessary at the time to maintain law and order. It punished offenders usually by fines, and did not have the power of putting people to death. Henry was interested in the securing of his power and this was carried out so well that the king became one of the wealthiest monarchs the country has ever had. He looked at the accounts himself and used to sign the pages after checking them, but it is not true to say that he was miserly because he could spend lavishly on court functions. He encouraged trade as Edward IV had done and took part in the geographical discoveries of the time. He financed the expeditions of John and Sebastian Cabot who set out from Bristol and discovered Newfoundland. This was an age of geographical discoveries, though Henry was not involved in the voyages of Columbus, Vasco da Gama and Magellan, some of the famous names of the time.

The period of the Yorkist kings and the Tudors saw people taking much more interest in the world around them. Scholars began to question the authority of the Church and gathered in Florence to study the classics.

In 1453 Constantinople had fallen to the Turks and many scholars had escaped to the West with their parchments, producing a revival of interest known as the Renaissance. In England this was noticeable in William Caxton's setting up of his printing press at Westminster. Learning became fashionable, led by the royal family who were all very well educated, and as the period continues into the sixteenth century, so we shall see some of the effects of the Renaissance on the politics of the time, notably the Reformation.

In 1509 Henry died and was succeeded by his seventeen-year-old son, who took the title of Henry VIII. There was no opposition to the new king. He united in himself the claims of both rival houses of York and Lancaster and was young, handsome and a sportsman. To increase his popularity, his father's two finance ministers, Empson and Dudley, were executed on a charge of treason. We shall hear more of the Dudley family in future pages. Also Henry immediately married Catherine of Aragon.

Henry saw himself as another Henry V and wanted to prove himself as a general. He attacked France and defeated the French at the Battle of the Spurs, capturing the towns of Thérouanne and Tournai. Meanwhile the Scots took advantage of Henry's absence in France and invaded England under James IV, but suffered an appalling defeat at Flodden Field, where the king and about ten thousand Scots were killed. Peace was made with both countries. During the campaign in France, a young cleric named Wolsey began his career, which was to lead him to the positions of archbishop of York, lord chancellor and papal legate, in other words the most powerful man at court and the subject of much jealousy from other courtiers.

Henry now tried to impress the king of France by a display of wealth. He met the king on what is known as the Field of the Cloth of Gold, but nothing definite came of the meeting and shortly afterwards Henry allied himself with the emperor.

Queen Catherine had one daughter, Mary, and no son. Henry was concerned that if there was no son to succeed, there would be a return to civil war. He therefore wanted to divorce her, but at this time only the pope could grant a divorce and he was a prisoner of Catherine's nephew, Charles. Wolsey was instructed to get the king a divorce, but, hoping one day to become pope himself, he did not want to upset the pope and cardinals at Rome. Wolsey was dismissed and retired to York. He was then arrested for high treason and died at Leicester on his way south to face the charge.

The papacy was unpopular in England and had lost the respect of the people. Large sums of money went to Rome and many clergy were seen to be very wealthy. Henry forbade all payments to Rome and made Cranmer archbishop of Canterbury. The authority of the pope in England was abolished and Cranmer put through the divorce of Henry and Catherine. The king immediately married Anne Boleyn who was to become mother of Elizabeth I.

Henry declared himself an English Catholic and an act of Parliament made him supreme head of the Church. Not everyone accepted Henry's supremacy, and Sir Thomas More, Wolsey's successor as lord chancellor, refused to swear to the Act of Supremacy and was executed. Meanwhile Henry was rapidly running short of finance and ordered Cromwell, who had succeeded Wolsey as the king's chief minister, to suppress first of all the smaller monasteries and then the larger and transfer their revenues to the crown. But it should be pointed out that Henry had declared himself an English Catholic and intended that this should be so for the population.

In the north of England the people were very angry at the suppression of the monasteries. Robert Aske, a lawyer, led a rising and marched on York. Thirty thousand men marched south, but Henry promised that everything would be put right and they returned home. Early the next year Henry took advantage of more troubles in the north to say that his promises were no longer binding and arrested and executed the leaders and many others.

Meanwhile Anne Boleyn had a daughter, Elizabeth, but no son, and so Henry had her executed on a trumped-up charge of treason and married Jane Seymour. She was the favourite wife of the six and her son was to be the future Edward VI. After Jane's death, Cromwell advised the king to marry Anne of Cleves with a view to helping the alliance with Germany and strengthening his position against the French. When they met Henry was very disappointed with her appearance and persuaded Parliament to let him divorce Anne. She liked England and remained here until her death. Cromwell was blamed for this divorce, and he was tried and executed for high treason. The king married Catherine Howard, but she too was executed on a charge of treason and the king married Catherine Parr who survived him.

War broke out again with Scotland and France. The Scots invaded and were defeated at Solway Moss. James V was so affected by the defeat that he died, leaving the throne to his infant daughter, Mary, Queen of Scots.

Henry invaded France and captured Boulogne, but he was now

getting old and suffered from an ulcerous leg. He had also become very stout, and in 1547 died leaving the throne to the nine-year-old Edward. Henry had arranged a council of sixteen to rule for the young prince, but on Henry's death Edward's uncle, the Duke of Somerset, was made protector, assisted by the other members. The young king was a precocious boy. He was well educated and showed signs of being very clever. As far as could be seen he had more conscience than his father, but no more kindness of heart, though he was very popular with the Londoners.

Somerset was protector during the first two years of the reign. He and Archbishop Cranmer vigorously carried out Protestant reforms of the Church. In 1549 the first English prayer book was published; by then the king was showing signs of himself being an extreme Protestant. Somerset attempted to force the Scots to marry their queen to Edward and defeated them at Pinkie. The Scots sent Mary to France, where she later married the *Dauphin*, heir to the French throne.

In 1549 the people of Norfolk rebelled under the leadership of Robert Kett and Somerset was replaced by John Dudley, grandson of Henry VII's finance minister. He took the title of Duke of Northumberland. Under his protectorship the destruction of monasteries continued, though some money was used to found schools – these are known as King Edward schools.

By 1553 it was clear that King Edward was dying, and Northumberland attempted to change the succession which should have gone to Princess Mary, the Roman Catholic daughter of Catherine of Aragon. Northumberland proclaimed Lady Jane Grey – Edward's cousin and the Duke's daughter-in-law – as queen on Edward's death, but Mary, who was in many ways a typical Tudor, summoned all loyal citizens to come to her help and entered London in triumph. Northumberland was executed but Lady Jane was confined to the Tower of London.

Queen Mary restored Roman Catholicism. The Protestant bishops, Cranmer, Latimer and Ridley, were imprisoned. All the acts of Parliament passed under Henry VIII against the pope were repealed. The queen's settlement of the religious problem would probably have been accepted by the population if she had not insisted on marrying Philip of Spain.

Sir Thomas Wyatt of Kent rose in rebellion with the people of that county and marched on London, but did not have general support. Queen Mary went down to the Guildhall, appealed to the citizens of London, and London Bridge was made secure. Wyatt crossed the Thames at Kingston, but was taken prisoner and sent to the Tower, where he and Lady Jane Grey were later executed. The queen then married Philip and began her attempt to force people to become Roman Catholics. Three hundred people were burnt in four years for not conforming, including Latimer and Ridley in 1555 and Archbishop Cranmer in 1556 – all three at Oxford.

Philip had visited England before this for his wedding and now visited a second time and persuaded Mary to declare war on France. This was a disastrous war and Calais, the last of the English possessions in France, was lost. Mary was heartbroken by this loss and by the fact that Philip had returned to Spain. Mary had lost all her early popularity and was hated in England and was suffering from a serious illness. Thus in 1558 she died leaving the throne to Princess Elizabeth.

Elizabeth I inherited a difficult position from her half-sister, but she was greeted with general enthusiasm. She kept Mary's council and added to it Sir William Cecil, who remained her chief adviser for nearly forty years.

Her first problem was to sort out the religious situation. In 1559 Parliament passed two acts. The first stated that the monarch was the supreme governor of the Church. This remains so to this day. The second stated that Edward VI's prayer book should be used and that everybody should attend the Church of England. A small fine was levied for non-attendance. The queen's intention was that outwardly all should agree to the setting up of the Church of England, but that opinion should be free. She was herself by nature a Protestant, but as in all things was careful about publicising her opinions.

As befits a member of the Tudor family she was highly educated and of above average intelligence. Her tutor had been Roger Ascham. She was fond of music and dancing and played the harpsichord well. She was proficient in Greek, Latin, French, Italian and Spanish.

The problem of Mary, Queen of Scots was to dominate English politics until the defeat of the Spanish Armada. Mary had returned to Scotland on the death of her French husband, but found that during her absence Scotland had turned to the Protestant faith as a result of the teachings of John Knox. The queen was permitted to hold Roman Catholic services in her palace chapel at Holyrood.

Some four years after her return she married her cousin, Henry Darnley. Their son later became James VI of Scots and James I of England. Darnley was very jealous of the attention the queen paid to her private secretary, David Rizzio, and had him assassinated. Darnley was mysteriously murdered and suspicion fell on Mary and Lord Bothwell. Bothwell was found not guilty but other Scottish nobles were not satisfied with the verdict. Bothwell had meanwhile married Mary. These lords defeated Mary at Carberry Hill and imprisoned her in Lochleven Castle and forced her to abdicate in favour of her baby son, James VI. Mary charmed her gaolers in Lochleven and escaped, but was defeated at Langside with Bothwell. Mary fled to England asking for help from Elizabeth. Elizabeth detained her in various castles for the next nineteen years. Bothwell fled to Denmark where he died, insane after a lengthy and cruel imprisonment.

Mary, in England, became the centre for various plots against Elizabeth. There were three of which the third, usually called the Babington Plot after its leader, led to Mary's execution. Anthony Babington plotted to kill Elizabeth and put Mary on the throne. Mary agreed, but the plot was discovered and Mary was imprisoned very strictly in Fotheringhay Castle. In the following trial Mary was found guilty and executed in 1587.

For many years English sailors had been attacking Spanish ships on their way from the New World laden with treasure. Many sailors were involved and showed themselves to be better seamen than the Spaniards. The most famous sailor, or pirate, as the Spanish would have said, was Francis Drake. He had already led several expeditions against Spanish shipping, probably encouraged by the queen, who certainly made a profit out of this privateering. During the years 1577 to 1580 Drake had led an expedition round the world in the *Golden Hind*. This was a very profitable voyage.

In 1587 Drake sailed with twenty-three ships into Cadiz

Harbour which had twelve Spanish galleys guarding it. Inside the harbour were eighty ships, which were attacked by Drake and Vice-Admiral William Borough. The wind dropped but Drake was able to destroy twenty-four (he claimed thirty-seven).

It was well known that the Spanish were preparing an armada of ships to invade England in order to avenge the death of Mary, Queen of Scots, and take revenge for the activities of Drake, Hawkins and Raleigh, some of the more famous sailors.

The Spanish collected together a fleet of 130 ships and twenty thousand soldiers besides sailors. The plan was to sail under the leadership of the Duke of Medina-Sidonia from Spain to Dunkirk. There the fleet would pick up thirty thousand soldiers under the command of the Duke of Parma. They sailed on 20 May 1588, and were sighted off the Lizard Point on 19 July. The news was taken to Drake at Plymouth where he was playing bowls with some of the other sea captains. Drake declared that there was time to finish the game and defeat the Spaniards too!

The Spanish fleet worked its way slowly up the Channel and the English fleet under the command of Lord Howard of Effingham managed during the night to put itself between the wind and the enemy and pursued the Spaniards. The fleet forced the Spanish to take refuge in Calais and Drake sent fireships in. The Spanish cut their cables and sailed north, fighting a sea battle at Gravelines. Bad weather then forced the Spanish to escape along the east coast of England and round the north of Scotland and Ireland. During the next year just fifty-two ships returned to Spain.

The reasons for this great victory are several. The Spanish fleet was built for transporting soldiers rather than fighting the English. The sailors were not used to the winds and tides of the North Sea and many ships were wrecked off Scotland and Ireland. The English had developed smaller and more manoeuvrable vessels than the Spanish and were better commanded.

The relief felt by the country after this victory was enormous and was directed at the queen. She had come to Tilbury to review her troops at the time of the Spanish Armada and made a famous speech. The victory gave people a pride in themselves. This produced a flowering in the arts. English literature reached new heights with Shakespeare, Spenser and Jonson, amongst many others, and in the musical world Byrd, Gibbons and Tallis were well known. Among painters, Nicholas Hilliard was a famous miniaturist.

Nevertheless, all was not as well as is sometimes suggested, and when Elizabeth eventually died in 1603 she left to her successor, James I, many problems. The Spanish war continued after 1588 very unsuccessfully. The queen had to put down the rebellion of a favourite young courtier, Lord Essex. He had been attempting to control the customary trouble in Ireland and had returned to England in disgrace.

In Parliament members were looking for more power and demanded that the queen put an end to monopolies. With her prestige from a long reign, Elizabeth was able to put off the inevitable clash between crown and Parliament which was to come under the Stuart kings. Towards the end of the reign the Puritans first came to notice. They held that the Reformation had not gone far enough and objected to bishops, set forms of prayers and kneeling during services. Many had been imprisoned in this reign.

In 1601 Parliament passed the First Regular Poor Law, which continued until 1834. Each parish had to appoint overseers with powers to raise local taxation for the housing and feeding of the deserving poor. In 1600 the East India Company was founded, and during the twenty years from 1583 various colonisation attempts were made including Sir Walter Raleigh's failure in Virginia.

After the execution of Essex it was clear that Elizabeth's health was beginning to fade. She was asked who was to succeed her when she fell ill in the winter of 1602, but refused to say. The younger Cecil had everything arranged for the succession of James I, which took place in March 1603.

Chapter V
CROWN VERSUS PARLIAMENT

James VI of Scotland and I of England rode slowly from Edinburgh to London so that his new subjects could see him and also so that he could take a good look at this much wealthier country that he had inherited. His claim to the throne was through Henry VII's daughter, Margaret, who had married James IV of Scots. The new king was an object of interest amongst his new subjects, many of whom would have heard of his dislike of 'the people', his fear of assassination and his theory of the divine right of kings to rule. Not many of them would have been able to remember a man as their ruler, it being fifty-six years since the death of Henry VIII. James was a clever man and knew it. He had written books and was often anxious to show off his learning.

He called a meeting of bishops and Puritans to try to settle the problems between them, but this conference, held at Hampton Court, was unable to agree on much except that a new translation of the Bible into English should be produced. This production is the well-known Authorised Version of the Bible.

Though James was personally popular, there were those who did not want him as king. The Roman Catholics failed to obtain religious toleration from the king and formed a plot led by Robert Catesby. This plot, known as the Gunpowder Plot, was an attempt to blow up the king and Parliament at the opening of the new session in November 1605. The plot was discovered when a letter was sent to Lord Monteagle warning him not to attend the meeting. James was shown the letter and ordered a search to be made in the vaults. There Guy Fawkes was found with thirty-six barrels of gunpowder ready to be lit. Some of the plotters were killed at Holbeach House in Northamptonshire, where they had fled after the discovery of the plot. These included Catesby. Others were captured, including Fawkes, and later executed, but it was the results which were most important. Very strict laws were passed against the Roman Catholics which were not finally repealed until 1829, and we still have an annual commemoration of the event.

As mentioned in Elizabeth's reign, there had been signs of a clash to come between monarch and Parliament. This began to be very noticeable during James's reign and was to reach a climax in the reign of his son, Charles.

The king's first Parliament demanded the right to freedom from arrest and refused to grant the king many supplies. James managed to govern without Parliament for seven years, using favourites such as the earl of Somerset and the Duke of Buckingham. Kings could manage without parliamentary grants if the country was at peace.

James's third Parliament of 1621 declared that it had the right to freedom of speech and to discuss matters of public interest and that its rights came from the people and not the king.

James raised money in all sorts of different ways through the Star Chamber, but in 1624 war broke out with Spain, which meant that Parliament had to be called to provide money to pay for it. Meanwhile James, in an attempt to raise money, had released Sir Walter Raleigh from prison. The king had imprisoned Sir Walter for involvement in a plot thirteen years earlier and now ordered him to sail for Guiana in search of gold, with orders not to attack any Spanish. The expedition was unsuccessful, and on his return Raleigh was executed for treason connected with the earlier plot against the king.

In Europe the Thirty Years War had broken out. This need not concern us, except to mention that James married his daughter Elizabeth to Frederick, Elector Palatine, and from them the Hanoverians were to make their claim to the throne.

Back in England many Puritans realised that they would never be allowed to worship as they wanted, and left the country. In 1620 a small band of them known as the Pilgrim Fathers sailed to America from Holland and founded New Plymouth.

In 1625 James I died and his second son Charles succeeded, his elder son Henry having died earlier in the reign. James, as has been said, was clever, but did not really understand that times were

England before the Norman Conquest

HADRIAN'S WALL

NORTHUMBRIA

· York

MERCIA

NORTH FOLK
(NORFOLK)

SOUTH FOLK
(SUFFOLK)

OFFA'S DYKE

WALES

London
·

WESSEX

KENT

WEST WALES

SUSSEX

changing and that he could not rule as the Tudors had done. Parliament was now becoming supreme in matters of religion and finance; James's relations with it were poor and so he usually relied on his favourites and neglected Parliament, which made it stronger. He seems to have thought that kings were responsible to God rather than to the people. James was never in favour of war and died a disappointed man in the middle of war with Spain, leaving a very difficult situation to his son.

The story of Charles I's reign is really the story of the struggle between king and Parliament and this began in the first session of Parliament. The members granted the king financial aid for the war and the usual tax on wine and merchandise which monarchs were given, but in this case only for a year. Charles felt insulted and refused to accept.

The war with Spain was very unsuccessful and Parliament refused to grant more money and was dissolved. The second Parliament of the reign was called, but met with no more success. Charles raised money by means of benevolences, a system of forced loans used under Edward IV. The king dissolved his second Parliament, but since England was at war with Spain and now also with France, Charles was forced to summon a third. The House of Commons drew up a petition stating its complaints and Charles accepted it as he was in serious need of money. Parliament was again dissolved and the king and his advisers ruled for eleven years without one, through the Star Chamber Court. Money was raised in many different ways and the country remained peaceful. Meanwhile, Charles's favourite, the Duke of Buckingham, had been assassinated at Portsmouth and William Wentworth became the king's chief adviser.

In 1634 the king imposed a ship money tax on the seaports and coastal counties to raise money for the defence of the country. The next year it was extended to all counties and John Hampden, a Buckinghamshire squire, refused to pay. He lost his case on a majority verdict of the judges, but all might yet have been well for Charles if, acting on Archbishop Laud's advice, he had not tried to force the English prayer book on the Scots. They formed protest groups against this action and Charles raised an army to attack them. His army proved untrustworthy and Charles had to agree to the Scots deciding their own religious future in the General Assembly. The Scots then invaded England and Charles dissolved his fourth Parliament for refusing to supply money to deal with the Scots.

Charles was now in a very weak position and was compelled to agree to pay the Scots eight hundred and fifty pounds for every day that they remained in England. The only answer for Charles was to call another Parliament in 1640 and this was the famous one known as the Long Parliament, as it lasted twenty years.

First this Parliament removed Wentworth and Laud from office and abolished the Star Chamber. The members then passed a bill declaring that Parliament could not be dissolved without their consent. Charles went down to the House and tried to have five members arrested, but failed as they had advance notice of the king's approach. The king then left the capital as Parliament was passing a bill limiting his power as king, especially as commander-in-chief of the army, and set up his headquarters at Oxford. Both sides prepared reluctantly for war.

In the war that followed the Royalists held the advantage to begin with as they had the better officers. Many of Charles's friends at court had had military experience in Europe and the king was able to call on his nephew, Prince Rupert of the Rhine, who was an experienced cavalry commander. The Royalists also had superior cavalry and were able to convert their assets into coin for the payment of troops more quickly than the Parliamentarians.

The Parliamentarians had long-term advantages. They held the navy and could control trade. They were supported by the merchant classes and London, whereas Charles's chief support came from the west and the north. It was clear to both sides that the king needed a quick victory, because the longer the war continued, the more likely a Parliamentarian victory would be. This was not to be a class war as both sides were mixed. The king's party received the name of Cavaliers and the opposition were called Roundheads.

The king commanded his army with Prince Rupert, the Duke of Newcastle, Hopton and Wilmot as his generals. On the Roundhead side the commander-in-chief was Lord Essex (son of

Elizabeth's favourite) and prominent generals included Manchester, Waller, Fairfax and Cromwell.

In 1642 the king's aim was to capture London and so he marched from Oxford and met Essex at Edgehill, not far from Banbury. Here an indecisive battle was fought, leaving the way open for the king to continue his march. However, the London trained bands came out to oppose Charles and he withdrew to Oxford, which remained his headquarters for the rest of the war. In 1643 Prince Rupert defeated and killed Hampden at Chalgrove Field, and in the north the earl of Fairfax was defeated. Bristol was taken by Rupert. Parliament also won enough victories this year to show that both sides were evenly matched, so each began to look round for allies. Charles made an alliance with the Irish and Parliament with the Scots. Cromwell meanwhile had formed and trained his Ironsides, his personal cavalry, and they were mainly responsible for the first decisive battle of the war. This was fought at Marston Moor, near York. Here the Duke of Manchester and Cromwell defeated the Duke of Newcastle and Rupert. By this defeat Charles lost control of the north.

Parliament was not satisfied that the generals were prosecuting the war against the Cavaliers as hard as they should and passed an act compelling all commanders to resign, but exempting Fairfax and Cromwell.

During the winter of 1644 Cromwell organised the New Model Army on the lines of his Ironsides. This was the foundation of a standing army and within six months had proved its effectiveness by defeating Charles at Naseby. This army was properly trained and paid. After his defeat at Naseby, Charles surrendered to the Scots, but in 1646 was handed over to Parliament. He was taken to Holmby House and then to Hampton Court, but escaped to Carisbrooke Castle on the Isle of Wight, where he was kept as a prisoner.

Meanwhile he plotted with the Scots, who invaded on his behalf, but were defeated by Cromwell at Preston. The army commanders returned to London and demanded the death of Charles. The king was brought to Westminster for trial, but refused to defend himself. He was tried by a specially formed court presided over by John Bradshaw and was found guilty of having waged war against his people and Parliament for which he was condemned and executed outside the Banqueting Hall in Whitehall in 1649. His body was taken to Windsor and buried next to Henry VIII in his vault in the choir of St George's Chapel, silently, with no service.

Prince Charles, eldest son of the late king, had fled to the continent and was proclaimed as Charles II by those who had fled with him, and the earl of Montrose rebelled on his behalf. Montrose was captured and executed by the Covenanters, who were those who had objected to Charles I's attempt to force the prayer book on them.

Charles II landed in Scotland and with General Leslie was defeated by Cromwell at Dunbar. Charles was crowned at Scone and invaded England. He evaded Cromwell, but was pursued and defeated at Worcester. After many romantic adventures Charles reached Brighton and escaped to France. General Monck was put in charge of Scotland. Meanwhile war had been declared against the Dutch. The English, under Admiral Blake, were defeated off the Naze by van Tromp, but in 1653 van Tromp was defeated and killed off the Texel and peace was signed.

Cromwell wanted to bring about some changes in the government. To do this he had to dissolve those members of the Long Parliament who still remained, the Rump as it is usually called. Cromwell was by now the most powerful and influential man in Britain and he summoned an assembly, called the Barebones Parliament after the first name on the list of members. This failed and so the military council under Cromwell drew up the Instrument of Government, which installed Oliver Cromwell as Lord Protector of the Commonwealth. He could call a Parliament and keep his army and the office of protector was to be his for life.

His first Parliament questioned his authority and was dissolved some months later. The Royalists were encouraged by these problems facing Cromwell to plot against him and so he divided the country into twelve areas under major generals.

War was now declared against Spain during which Jamaica was taken and Blake captured the Spanish silver fleet off Cadiz and later defeated them at Tenerife. France now joined in but the New

Model Army defeated the Spanish at the Dunes and captured Dunkirk.

Cromwell needed money for this war and called a Parliament. This assembly practically restored the old constitution of Britain as it offered Cromwell the crown. He refused the title but accepted the power of nominating his successor and agreed to having a second House of Parliament. Cromwell's third Parliament refused to accept the Upper House and was dissolved and Cromwell ruled for the rest of his life without a Parliament. The parallel with events in Charles I's reign is very noticeable.

On 3 September 1658, which happened to be the anniversary of his great victories at Dunbar and Worcester, Cromwell died and was buried in Westminster Abbey. His son, Richard Cromwell, was declared protector, but soon after his election he resigned and retired into private life.

It was obvious to many people by now that the only solution to the problem of government was the restoration of the Stuart kings in the person of Charles II. The Rump was recalled by the army, but tried to bring the army under its control and so was dismissed by General Lambert. General Monck now marched south with his troops and many soldiers deserted Lambert to join Monck, who entered London and recalled the Long Parliament. This dissolved itself and called a convention which had many Royalists amongst its members.

The convention passed a resolution restoring the old form of government and asking Charles to return. Charles had been secretly corresponding with General Monck and now issued the Declaration of Breda, which promised a general pardon and payment of money owing to the army and some freedom in religious matters. He was then restored to the throne and entered London on 30 May 1660, his thirtieth birthday, and the Puritan experiment in government was over.

Chapter VI
RESTORATION ENGLAND

Charles II was received in England with extraordinary enthusiasm. However, few of the problems of his father's reign or of the Commonwealth had been solved. The convention which had recalled him passed several laws. These allowed all those involved in offences committed under Cromwell, except those responsible for the execution of Charles I, to be pardoned. The king's income was settled as a sum for life and the army was disbanded except for two regiments. The Church and a few Cavaliers had their lands restored. Some of these Cavaliers were the founders of the modern Tory party, and those Roundheads who held on to their lands became the founders of the Whig or Liberal party as it became known. The king then dissolved the convention and called a Parliament.

Meanwhile war had broken out again with the Dutch and was very unsuccessful. The navy was unable to stop the Dutch from sailing up the Thames and blockading Chatham. Gunfire was heard in the capital. This was the third year of disasters. Two years before in 1665 plague broke out in London, lasting from May to September and killing about one hundred thousand people, one in six of the capital's population. (These figures are approximate.) The year following, during a very dry and hot summer, the Great Fire raged for almost a week in July destroying two-thirds of the city.

These disasters and Charles's attitude to government resulted in the early enthusiasm for him going, though he was usually able to ensure that his ministers took the blame for disasters and misgovernment. He himself was in correspondence with Louis XIV of France in an attempt to be given a pension which would enable him to rule without Parliament. In return he would declare

Britain a Roman Catholic country. The heir to the throne, Charles's brother, James, was to be excluded from his title. Charles refused to accept this and always remained loyal to his brother.

A third Dutch war was fought, little more successful than the others, and when peace was signed James's daughter Mary was married to the Dutch Stadtholder, William of Orange.

Meanwhile, a certain Titus Oates had disclosed a plot against the king by the Roman Catholics. He said that the murder of the king was planned and that the Roman Catholic religion was to be restored. National hysteria resulted and many Roman Catholics were imprisoned and London put in a state of siege with the trained bands called out, but gradually feelings calmed down.

The opposition in the House of Commons, now being called Whigs, believed that a plan was being thought up to allow in the Roman Catholics and in 1681 came to Parliament bringing armed followers with them and Britain seemed to be heading for civil war again.

A bid to exclude James from the succession was announced, but Charles dissolved Parliament before the bill was passed and the violent conduct of the Whigs resulted in a Tory reaction. The nation again came to the support of the king.

The Whigs plotted to assassinate Charles when he was on his way back from Newmarket races at a lonely farmhouse called Rye House. The plot was disclosed and Charles escaped. He was now so popular as the 'Merry Monarch' that he was able to govern for the last four years of his life without a Parliament.

On his deathbed in 1685 he did two characteristic things. He became a Roman Catholic himself and apologised to those around him for being such an unconscionably long time dying! Charles can be described as the most successful of the Stuart kings, and once said that his brother James would not remain king for long, and the events of the next three years were to prove him right.

James II succeeded without any difficulty, partly because of his brother's popularity and partly because he stated in his accession address that he would keep the government and the Church as established by law.

Those Whigs who had been exiled for their part in the Rye House Plot planned a rebellion, the object of which was to dethrone the king and crown the Duke of Monmouth – an illegitimate son of Charles II. Monmouth landed at Lyme and was proclaimed king at Taunton. At Sedgemoor he attempted a night attack on the king's forces and was defeated. He was captured while hiding in a ditch and taken to London, where he had no mercy from his uncle and was executed. Judge Jeffreys was sent to the West Country to deal with those who had rebelled and hanged 320 and had 840 transported to colonies overseas.

James's aims were twofold. He wanted to be able to rule without Parliament and restore the Roman Catholic religion. The ease with which he had defeated Monmouth encouraged him in his aims and so he formed and kept a large army on Hounslow Heath to overawe London and claimed the right to do without the laws of the country. He began to appoint Roman Catholics to positions of authority in the army and universities.

These points were generally accepted, but he then ordered the clergy to read on two Sundays in 1688 a Declaration of Indulgence. This suspended all penal laws against Roman Catholics and Non-conformists. The clergy mostly refused and seven bishops petitioned the king in person to be excused from reading it. They were imprisoned in the Tower and tried but to the great excitement of the Londoners were acquitted.

All these things might have been grudgingly accepted, but in July 1688 a son was born to the queen. There was doubt in the country about the authenticity of the boy's birth and it was rumoured that he had been brought into the palace in a warming pan. This would mean the accession of another Roman Catholic, rather than the Protestant Princess Mary, James II's elder daughter.

Seven influential Whigs and Tories sent a letter to William and Mary in Holland asking them to come over with an army and defend England against the king. James tried to reverse the things he had been doing but it was too late. On 5 November William landed at Torbay and marched slowly towards London. James fled for France, dropping the Great Seal in the Thames, and William arrived in the capital. A convention met and after long discussion decided to offer the crown to William and Mary. This was written into the Declaration of Rights of 1689. William and Mary accepted, and after being declared king and queen were crowned jointly in Westminster Abbey.

The first act of the new reign was to turn the convention into a Parliament, which passed some important bills. As a result of these Parliament took complete control of the army. The king could no longer dispense with the law or levy money without its consent, or keep a standing army in time of peace without parliamentary agreement. It was also agreed that Parliament should meet frequently.

There was considerable opposition to the new arrangement for William was never a popular monarch until the last few months of his reign. In Scotland Viscount Dundee defeated the royal forces at Killiecrankie. William called all the Highland chieftains to take the oath of allegiance to him and his queen, but MacDonald of Glencoe did not reach Inverness by 1 January 1692, the date for taking the oath. The secretary for Scotland obtained a royal warrant to punish the MacDonalds and sent in the Campbells, their hereditary enemies, to carry out the sentence and nearly the whole clan was massacred.

In Ireland James II attempted to regain his throne and came over from France to rule in Dublin. The Protestants in London-derry were besieged by the Roman Catholics for three months, until relief arrived from London.

William invaded Ireland and defeated James at the Battle of the Boyne. James fled to France. William subdued the south of Ireland and many Irish soldiers escaped to France and joined the armies of Louis XIV. William had spent most of his adult life fighting the French in defence of Holland. War now broke out again with the French and they suffered a great naval defeat off La Hogue. William took the fortress of Namur and peace was concluded, with William being acknowledged as king.

Meanwhile it had become clear that William's sister-in-law and successor, Anne, would have no surviving children and a succession act was necessary. Its main object was to ensure that the throne remained Protestant and so a law was passed which said that Sophia, granddaughter of James I, should succeed after Anne. This act excluded the son born to James II in 1688 on the grounds that he was being brought up as a Roman Catholic.

The king of Spain was very ill and had no children, and by his will he had left Spain to the French king's grandson, Philip of Anjou. William could see that the potential uniting of France and Spain would upset all the work he had put into defending Holland. England, Holland and Austria formed an alliance to exclude Philip.

In 1701 James II died in France and Louis XIV declared his son, James, the boy born in 1688, rightful king of England. William dissolved Parliament and the new Parliament declared war against France. This war, usually known as the War of the Spanish Succession, was popular, as was William now. However, in 1702, while out riding in Hampton Court grounds, he fell from his horse and died some days later from the effects of the fall, but not before recommending to Anne that she appoint John Churchill to command the army.

It should be noted that during this important reign two financial systems began. The National Debt was begun to help with the costs of the French war. Unlike other debts, only the interest is paid, and also the Bank of England was established. A Scotsman, William Paterson, had suggested the idea and it was taken up, whereby lenders were formed into a company which did all its business with the government and were paid interest on their money. This bank was a great success and its security has become a proverb.

Parliament passed a bill limiting its own duration to three years and also stating that it must be called within three years. Queen Mary had died some years before William and no children had survived, so in 1702 Mary's sister came to the throne as Queen Anne. Queen Anne promptly appointed John Churchill as commander of the army and the allies then agreed to his commanding all their armies. The war began quietly, though the fortress town of Liège was taken.

In 1704 Churchill planned to relieve Vienna from French attack. The Dutch would not allow him to take their troops out of their country, so he marched down the Moselle, then up the Rhine to Mainz and was then far enough away from Holland to strike rapidly across Germany. He crossed the Danube and was joined by troops under Prince Eugene. The allies were now between the French and Vienna and faced the united forces of the French and Bavarians under Marshal Tallard at the village of Blenheim. Here

Churchill, now Duke of Marlborough, won an extraordinary victory in which two-thirds of the French army were either killed, wounded or taken prisoner. Marshal Tallard was also captured. This victory saved Austria, and Marlborough was rewarded with a pension and the estate and palace of Blenheim. This year also saw the capture of Gibraltar.

Two years later Marlborough again defeated the French, this time at Ramillies in the Netherlands. The same thing happened two years later at Oudenarde near the French border. The next year Marlborough invaded France and defeated the French at Malplaquet, but with such heavy losses that there were calls for the end of war and the government of the Whigs fell. This resulted in a Tory administration and the end of the war. Marlborough was accused of misusing public money and dismissed, and was not given his posts back until the next reign.

In 1713 a treaty was signed which stated that the French and Spanish thrones should never be united, that England was to keep Gibraltar and that France should acknowledge the Protestant succession in England. During this reign England and Scotland were finally united by an act of Parliament and were to be called Great Britain. The two countries were to be governed by one Parliament, but Scotland could keep its Church, laws and courts of justice.

Queen Anne had a sad life, losing all her many children and being under the influence of two ladies – first the duchess of Marlborough, then, when the government changed in 1711, a Mrs Masham; but during her reign the country's reputation abroad had never stood higher thanks to the victories of Marlborough.

In 1714 Queen Anne, the last of the Stuart family to reign in Britain, died, and was succeeded by George I, the first Hanoverian.

Chapter VII

THE YEARS OF EMPIRE

The eighteenth century began with war, and fighting was to continue throughout most of its duration, but the period which actually saw the accession of George I was comparatively peaceful.

Queen Anne had died without any of her seventeen children surviving her, and so, to keep the idea of a Protestant monarchy, the succession had been placed on Sophia, granddaughter of James I and youngest daughter of Elizabeth, James's daughter. George was Sophia's son and so succeeded in 1714, his mother having died earlier that year. George was a Hanoverian and spoke little or no English, so the government tended to be in the hands of his ministers. We see here the beginnings of the idea that the king reigns rather than rules. This meant that the real power lay with the prime minister and the government of the day. The king or queen now became merely an influential figurehead.

At the beginning of this chapter it was stated that this reign was a peaceful one, but there were some wars which attempted to keep the balance of power in Europe. England sent Admiral Byng to protect Sicily, which Philip of Spain was attacking. The admiral completely destroyed the Spanish fleet off Cape Passaro. Spain made peace and renounced all claims to the French throne.

Back in London there was a very remarkable financial scandal. The directors of the South Sea Company offered to pay off part of the National Debt if they could have the exclusive right to all trading in the South Seas. This was agreed and thousands of people thought that the company must be safe to invest in. It was not, as was soon discovered, and the South Sea Bubble, as this affair is called, soon burst, ruining many hundreds.

Sir Robert Walpole restored confidence and considerable credit and thereby placed himself in power as the first lord of the

Treasury for over twenty years. He is sometimes known as the first prime minister, and his time as chief minister covers parts of the reigns of the first two Hanoverians. Walpole was a fine debater in the House of Commons and an excellent handler of people. His main policy was to keep Britain out of war and in this he was greatly supported by Queen Caroline, wife of George II. The country needed time to recover from the wars of the early years of the century and Walpole's financial measures began slowly to reduce the National Debt. Walpole was not averse to taking bribes. He also increased trade in the Mediterranean. He assured that the succession should remain in Hanoverian hands and left Britain wealthy, wealth that was to be used in the next wars.

Before attempting to deal with these wars, we should look at the Jacobite rebellions. These were attempts by the Stuart pretenders, James II's descendants. They were both centred in the Highlands, and in both cases risings in England failed because people had become used to settled life under the early Georges and did not want to have anything to do with Scottish attempts to force a king on them.

The rebellion of 1715 was led by the earl of Mar in Scotland and by a Mr Forster in Lancashire. It was intended that Irish contingents should land in the west. The Scots were defeated at Sheriffmuir by the Duke of Argyll. At Preston, on the same day, Mr Forster surrendered. All this took place before the Old Pretender had even landed. When he did he seemed so uninspiring in the face of prompt English action that he decided to return to France. Some of the leaders were imprisoned in the Tower of London, but one of them, Lord Nithsdale, escaped dressed in his wife's gown, along with Mr Forster.

The second rebellion took place in 1745, during the War of the Austrian Succession, and was well-timed by the Jacobites because English troops were on the Continent. They had just defeated the French at Dettingen and had been led in battle by George II himself, the last time a British king led his troops into battle. This war roused the Jacobites to try once more to put the Old Pretender on the throne. His son, Bonnie Prince Charlie, landed with seven men and called on the Scots to rally round him at Glenfinnan. About twelve thousand did so and he marched on Edinburgh, which he captured except for the castle. He then defeated a small force under General Cope at Prestonpans and invaded England. He marched down the west coast and then turned inland to Derby, reaching there on Friday, 4 December. Here his council persuaded him that his forces were not strong enough to continue south and so he very reluctantly began his retreat. Along the way he lost many by desertion, but won a battle at Falkirk though he continued the retreat.

Meanwhile British troops were returning from the continent under the Duke of Cumberland, George II's son, and Charles was completely defeated at Culloden Moor in April 1746. The prince managed to escape from the place where he had landed the year before after five months of wandering through the Highlands and reached France.

Cumberland was nicknamed 'Butcher' Cumberland for the way he treated the Scots after the battle and thousands emigrated to America. The Highlanders were disarmed and forbidden to wear their national dress, but the country did settle down and within thirteen years Scottish regiments were present at the victory of Quebec under General Wolfe.

Peace was signed in 1748 but most people seemed to think that this was merely a break between campaigns in Europe as the problem of which nation would be pre-eminent had not been solved. Also we should note that France and England were competing for colonies in India and America.

The war which was to break out in 1756, and which is usually called the Seven Years War, was the first one which Britain was to fight on a truly global scale. There were campaigns in Europe, America and India as well as naval warfare. The war in Europe began badly. Admiral Byng, son of the victor of Passaro, was sent to relieve Minorca, which the French were attacking, but he failed and withdrew. There was such an outcry in England at this that he was court-martialled and shot on his own quarterdeck. Then the Duke of Cumberland was defeated and surrendered at Kloster-zeven. He was recalled and Ferdinand of Brunswick took command.

To run a war of such complexity required a politician of genius and the country found one in William Pitt, secretary of state to the prime minister, the Duke of Newcastle. Pitt was a very remarkable man who could see how the various parts of the war affected each other. The combination of Newcastle finding the money and Pitt running the war turned into a very successful one. Pitt too was talented in finding the right men for the various posts of command from a small number of candidates.

The most successful year was to be 1759. The French were defeated at Minden by Ferdinand. Off Lagos, Admiral Boscawen defeated the French and Admiral Hawke did the same in Quiberon Bay. In Canada General Wolfe captured Quebec. In North America General Braddock was sent out to assist the colonists against the French General Montcalm, but was defeated at Fort Duquesne and killed. Pitt appointed General James Wolfe to command in Canada with instructions to drive the French out of that country.

The key to this campaign was the capture of Quebec, then held by the French. Wolfe failed to force the city into surrender by bombardment and so looked for ways of taking his troops across the St Lawrence River. This he succeeded in doing and his advance guard found a path up the cliffs to the Heights of Abraham, an area outside Quebec. Here he defeated Montcalm, but was himself killed during the battle. Montcalm died of his wounds the next day. The capture of Quebec put an end to French power in Canada.

Meanwhile, in India three years before, the Black Hole of Calcutta incident had occurred, where 146 English prisoners had been confined in the narrow guardroom of the garrison by the Nawab of Bengal, soon after he seized Calcutta. Only twenty-three were found alive the next day. Robert Clive, who had come out to India as a bank clerk, was sent to punish the Nawab. He retook Calcutta and then at Plassey defeated the Nawab's much larger army, securing Bengal for Britain. By 1760 French power no longer existed in India. Pitt wanted to extend the war, but the rest of his ministers refused and he resigned. War was, however, declared on Spain, and Havana and Manila were captured.

Both sides were now exhausted from the war and negotiations for peace were begun, ending in the Treaty of Paris. By this treaty England kept its conquests except for some of the islands in the West Indies and restored some trading posts in India to France.

This war was successful on land and sea and brought Britain its first empire and a great statesman in William Pitt, earl of Chatham.

Meanwhile across the Atlantic relations with the American colonies were deteriorating. England governed them on the theory that colonies existed for the benefit of the mother country. The war in Europe which had just finished had added millions to the National Debt and had to be paid for, and so it was proposed that money should be obtained from the colonists by a Stamp Act or charge on contracts and wills. The act was passed, but some of the colonies declared that taxation without their consent was illegal and this opposition persuaded the government to repeal the act.

The chancellor of the Exchequer, in the absence of the prime minister, Pitt, through ill health, passed a new tax imposing duties on tea and other articles imported into America. A number of colonists, dressed and painted as Red Indians, boarded the tea ships in Boston Harbour and emptied all the tea-chests into the sea.

The English government responded by closing Boston Harbour. War followed, beginning with an indecisive battle at Lexington near Boston. The English removed the colonists from Bunker's Hill above Boston after some very harsh fighting. At this point in the war, the colonists appointed George Washington as their commander and the English under General Howe were forced to evacuate Boston. This was in 1776.

On 4 July 1776 the American Congress of the original thirteen states declared independence. During the next year there came the turning point of the war for the colonists, when Washington forced General Burgoyne to surrender at Saratoga Springs. France and Spain now joined in on the side of the colonists hoping for revenge for their losses in the previous war and England stood alone. Two years later Lord Cornwallis was compelled to surrender at Yorktown and the war was over, though not without Admiral Rodney winning two victories at sea, one over the Spanish off Cape St Vincent and the other over the French off St Lucia. A treaty was signed at Versailles by which England gave the American colonies their independence.

It is often asked why the English lost to a much smaller number of colonists, and the answer lies in several reasons. The colonists produced in Washington the best general on either side. The fact that France and Spain joined in made the odds too great and the distance between London and the war zone made running the war virtually impossible. Also the English underestimated the Americans and had no war minister of Pitt's type to organise the campaign. The very next year after the end of the war George III called on Pitt the Younger, second son of the great war minister, to become prime minister at the age of twenty-four.

Before continuing with the political history of the eighteenth century, we should look briefly at some of the changes taking place during the years of the Industrial Revolution.

In agriculture, farmers were enclosing their land with hedges and fences, because they found themselves handicapped by the old method of strip farming. Among the many pioneers of agriculture was Jethro Tull, who published a book on farming in 1733 and invented a plough and a seed drill by which seeds could be planted in rows. Lord Townshend introduced on his estates fourfold rotation by cultivating turnips, which also provided winter food for his cattle. Thus many farmers could feed their herds during the winter. Robert Bakewell experimented in the breeding of larger cattle and sheep, more than doubling their weight. The population began to grow rapidly. It was about nine million in 1800 and by 1881 was reckoned at twenty-six million.

The great age of canal building came in the late eighteenth century. The pioneer here was James Brindley. He built three hundred miles of canal though he never learnt to write, solving problems by going to bed and thinking them out.

Road improvements took place seriously for the first time since the Roman occupation. Blind Jack Metcalf was a great walker and used to guide people over the moors at Harrogate. He contracted to build a road in 1765. Thomas Telford was a Scotsman and began by building bridges. He then moved to road building using flat stones instead of jagged ones. His roads wore well and in 1815 he began work on the London to Holyhead road – the present A5 – which was completed in 1830 and for which he built the Menai Bridge. His roads were very expensive. John Macadam devised a much cheaper method. He did not use a foundation of large stones but a layer of about ten inches of small stones laid directly on the ground, consisting mainly of limestone and sandstone. These slowly ground away and filled any cracks. The powder combined with rain and became a sort of concrete. By 1820 the country was being covered with a network of fine roads, and where in 1750 it took sixteen days to travel from London to Edinburgh, in 1830 the journey could be done in forty hours.

There are many other names to be mentioned as Britain led the world in the Industrial Revolution. Among the more famous were Richard Arkwright, inventor of the spinning frame for cotton mills, who set up the first cotton mill in England at Matlock. Josiah Wedgwood greatly improved the manufacture of porcelain and invented the queen's ware. James Watt was a famous engineer and developed steam power. John Smeaton built the Eddystone Lighthouse. In medicine Edward Jenner discovered the method of vaccination for preventing smallpox. James Cook, who had led General Wolfe up the St Lawrence at the time of the Battle of Quebec, sailed twice round the world and on the third time was killed by natives in the Sandwich Islands. The list of names is long and we shall come back to it in Victorian times with the arrival of the railway age.

Now we go abroad to look briefly at the French Revolution. The differences between the privileged and unprivileged were much greater in France than in Britain. Many Frenchmen had fought as volunteers with the Americans and had returned to France full of enthusiasm for liberty. The French government was showing itself to be extremely inefficient in paying its way and so Louis XVI summoned the States-General, their Parliament, after an interval of 175 years. The Commons declared themselves a National Assembly and overthrew the government. Riots broke out in Paris and the mob attacked and demolished the Bastille, the great state prison in the city. The assembly then abolished all the rights which the nobility and clergy held. The king and his family attempted to escape from France and reached Varennes but were recognised and brought back to Paris. France was declared a republic when Austria and Prussia invaded in an attempt to restore the monarchy, but were stopped at Valmy. Louis XVI was tried and executed in 1793 and Queen Marie Antoinette the next year. Many hundreds of the nobility were guillotined the same year and the Republic offered help to all those nations who wanted to overthrow their kings. Pitt declared war on France.

The war began well on both land and sea, though this situation was not to continue on land. At sea Lord Howe won a great victory off Brest and Admiral Jervis defeated the Spanish off Cape St Vincent while Admiral Duncan defeated the Dutch off Camperdown. On land a young Corsican, Napoleon Bonaparte, had saved the French Republic by recapturing Toulon and had then defeated the Austrians and captured northern Italy. He then invaded Egypt aiming possibly at the capture of India. Rear Admiral Nelson was sent to attack the French fleet and destroyed eleven out of thirteen ships at the Battle of the Nile. Later the French army in Egypt surrendered. Nelson also took Malta at this time.

In Europe the northern countries formed an armed neutrality against British claims to search all ships. Admiral Hyde Parker, with Nelson as second in command, destroyed the Danish fleet in Copenhagen Harbour. This battle was famous for the blind eye incident where Nelson put his telescope to his blind eye and said that he really could not see Admiral Parker's order to withdraw his ships. Nelson was then sent to blockade the French off Toulon and in 1805 totally defeated the combined French and Spanish fleets near Cape Trafalgar on 21 October, but was mortally wounded during the course of the action. His body was brought back to Britain and buried in St Paul's Cathedral after a state funeral.

The result of this battle was that the navy had command of the seas and so there was no further danger of invasion. However, on land Napoleon continued to dominate and was to do so for nearly ten more years.

Peace had been declared after the Battle of Copenhagen and Pitt resigned office, but, on his returning to Downing Street, war resumed in 1805, which led to the victory of Trafalgar, but serious defeats on land for the allies. Napoleon crushed the allied armies of Austria and Russia at Austerlitz. The news of this battle is said to have killed Pitt, who died shortly after.

Napoleon knew that Britain's strength lay in its trade and so tried to blockade this country, forbidding anybody to accept its trade. Portugal refused to obey these decrees and the French invaded, conferring the crown of Spain on Napoleon's brother. The people of the Peninsula rose against the French and appealed for help. This was continued for six years under first of all Sir Arthur Wellesley, later ennobled as the Duke of Wellington, then Sir John Moore, and, when he was killed at Corunna, Wellington again. In 1809 Wellington defeated the French at Talavera and built the lines of Torres Vedras north of Lisbon. Two frontier forts between Portugal and Spain, called Badajoz and Ciudad Rodrigo, were taken and Wellington advanced into Spain. Madrid was taken in 1812 and the next year Wellington was in the Pyrenees taking the war on to French soil and defeating them at Toulouse.

Meanwhile Napoleon had withdrawn troops for the invasion of Russia. He took some six hundred thousand men but discovered, as all would-be conquerors of that land have found, that it was too large to hold. He marched for some months towards Moscow with the Russians retreating and burning everything in his path. An indecisive battle was fought at Borodino near the capital and Napoleon entered the city expecting a surrender, but instead the Russians set fire to Moscow and the French were forced to retreat. The retreat began well except that the French had to recross the battlefield of Borodino; but soon the dreadful Russian winter set in and the French struggled through that for hundreds of miles. They had never expected to be retreating in the winter and were very poorly equipped to face the snows. The Russian Cossacks attacked the retreating army. Napoleon left the rearguard under the command of Marshal Ney and sped back to Paris. Here he raised yet another army, for he had lost about four hundred thousand men in Russia, and met the allies at Leipzig. After three days of very hard fighting he was defeated, and the allies invaded France, entering Paris. Napoleon abdicated and was exiled to Elba.

The allies convened a congress at Vienna to draw up a peace treaty, but their discussions were interrupted by the news that Napoleon had escaped and was marching on Paris, having landed in the south of France. He called on the army for their support. The allies decided to send large contingents of soldiers to defeat him. These were all put under the command of Wellington.

Napoleon defeated the Prussians at Ligny but on the same day Wellington was successful against Marshal Ney at Quatre Bras. The next day at Waterloo, twenty-one miles south of Brussels,

Napoleon and Wellington met for the first time in battle. The allied side waited for the French to attack and held them throughout the day until about 4 p.m. when Napoleon sent in the cavalry under Marshal Ney; but it was too late as the Prussians were now arriving on the battlefield in ever-increasing numbers. At 8 p.m. Napoleon sent in the Imperial Guard, his best troops, in two columns against the British right and centre, but failed to break through. The Guards were ordered to charge and broke the Imperial Guard and a general advance was ordered. The French were driven off the battlefield.

Napoleon fled to Paris and abdicated in favour of his son, but, finding escape from France impossible, gave himself up to the captain of HMS *Bellerophon* and was condemned to exile on the island of St Helena, where he stayed until he died in 1821.

The Battle of Waterloo (1815) came at the end of a long war, which itself was a continuation of all the wars of the eighteenth century; but one of the results was to be the longest period of peace in Europe since probably the time of the Roman occupation. The war had left Britain without a rival as a colonial power and unchallenged at sea.

It may have been noticed that since the arrival of the Hanoverians, kings have not featured much in our story as power had now passed to the Lords and Commons. Waterloo came towards the end of a very long and popular reign, that of George III. Unfortunately, for the last nine years of his life he suffered from porphyria, an illness which produces mental instability, and his son, later George IV, became regent, though his father's insanity did not diminish the king's popularity.

In 1820 he died and was succeeded by George IV for ten years and then George IV's brother, William IV, was king for seven years. These were years of discontent, for the wars had to be paid for and taxes rose. Harvests were bad and trade took a long time to recover after the wars. Parliament passed laws forbidding the import of corn, so prices at home rose. This led to riots and to a demand for the reform of Parliament. Fear of revolution had kept the Tories, first mentioned in Charles II's reign, from reforming Parliament, but in 1830 the Whigs were returned and set about many reforms.

Some changes in the distribution of seats in the Commons were made in 1832. After great excitement in the country and an unsuccessful attempt by King William to hinder it, the electorate was enlarged by about half a million. Many seats in Parliament were owned by the great landowners or had very few voters. Old Sarum had no votes at all. These seats were called rotten boroughs and many were removed. Their seats were given to the growing towns of the country. This reform was followed by the Abolition of Slavery Act in all British lands and a Factory Act which stated that children under nine should not work in factories. The hours for under-thirteens were limited to eight a day. A Poor Law made it illegal for any able-bodied man to have financial relief unless he lived in a workhouse, though relief of bread was still granted.

Towards the end of William IV's reign an act was passed for local government. Every borough with a population of over ten thousand was to have a town council and publish its accounts. By another act, Parliament granted societies money to provide some sort of elementary education and an act of 1829 gave religious toleration to Roman Catholics. In the middle of all this reforming zeal, William IV died and his niece Victoria succeeded, and so we have reached the Victorian Age.

Queen Victoria was only eighteen when she succeeded her uncle in 1837. Her court was a cheerful one and in 1840 she married her cousin, Prince Albert, and in time had nine children.

This reign is a study in itself, so we shall look at certain incidents in it, rather than try to cover it all. First this was the beginning of the railway age. Railway tracks were known in the early seventeenth century. They were wooden and vans on them were pulled by horses. Newcomen was the first man to apply steam power when he designed a beam engine in 1712. James Watt and Richard Trevithick built improved engines which were stationary, but George Stephenson built the first practical steam locomotive and his work was carried on by his son, Robert. George Stephenson won the Rainhill Trials in 1829 with the *Rocket* and the first regular passenger service was on the Liverpool to Manchester line. The queen travelled by rail for the first time in 1842 and the age of railways had begun, with most of the existing great railway lines established between 1835 and 1850.

In Europe the year 1848 saw revolutions in many countries and the French king, Louis Philippe, fled to Britain. A republic was again established in France. In Britain demonstrations took place in an attempt to make changes in the government. These were the Chartist risings, but a big march in London was a failure and it became clear that changes would have to be brought about by legal means.

In 1851 the Great Exhibition was held. This was Prince Albert's idea and took place in London in the Crystal Palace. Its object was to show British manufacturers that they could improve their own work by comparing it with that of foreign nations and to show where industry in the world had reached. The exhibition was a great success.

There had been comparative peace in Europe for forty years, but in 1854 war broke out in the Crimea. An argument had arisen between Russia and Turkey over who should guard the holy places in Jerusalem. The Tsar, Nicholas I, claimed the right to protect all Christians living under Turkish rule, and, as with most Russian rulers, wanted to extend his own lands as far as Constantinople because he desperately needed the Black Sea warm water ports. His only coastlines in the north were frozen solid for six months of the year. Britain, France, Austria and Prussia suggested to the Sultan that he should accept the Russian demands, but he refused and Nicholas I invaded Turkey. Britain and France came to the help of the Sultan and declared war on Russia. Meanwhile the Russian fleet destroyed the Turkish ships at Sinope, so the allies sent their fleet and armies to attack Sebastopol, the great Russian naval base.

Lord Raglan defeated the Russians at the crossing of the River Alma, but the French refused to follow up the defeat and the war dragged on into the winter as the allies besieged Sebastopol. Before winter really set in, the Battle of Balaclava was fought. Lord Cardigan received an order, which he misinterpreted, to attack the Russian guns through a valley lined by Russian troops. Six hundred of the Light Brigade rode through and reached the guns. Only a few returned, including Lord Cardigan.

During the winter the troops suffered from lack of food and shelter through bad management. The hospital services were appalling, until Florence Nightingale came out and reorganised the medical services at Scutari. Previous wars had been badly managed, but William Russell, *The Times*'s correspondent, sent back by the new telegraph system such remarkable accounts of the troops' suffering that the government of Lord Aberdeen fell and Lord Palmerston became prime minister. He and his government pushed on the war much more vigorously. A railway was built from Balaclava to the camp to supply the troops with provisions and the result was the fall of Sebastopol. Nicholas I died and his successor gave the allies all they demanded. Queen Victoria instituted the Victoria Cross made from metal captured from Russian guns. Florence Nightingale became the heroine of the war bringing comfort and help to the soldiers as the Lady with the Lamp. She continued her work for the medical services throughout her long life, opening a school of nursing at St Thomas's Hospital and working hard on nursing reform schemes. In 1907 she was awarded the Order of Merit.

In another part of the world, namely India, trouble broke out as the Crimean War came to a close. The reasons are several. Much irritation was caused amongst the natives in the province of Oudh when the territory was taken over by the British. Native sepoy troops objected to serving overseas because this led to loss of caste. The British treatment of native troops was poor, often contemptible, and it was widely believed that it was intended to force Christianity on them. The British wanted to abolish many native customs, in particular suttee, the custom whereby at a cremation the widow was burnt too. A rumour went round among the troops that the new cartridges recently issued were coated in cow and pig fat. The cow was sacred to the Hindu and the pig unclean to the Muslim. These cartridges had to be bitten before use, therefore upsetting the main faiths in the sepoy regiments. There was also a widespread belief that British rule would last only a hundred years from the Battle of Plassey, 1757. This date had now arrived.

The mutiny was limited to Bengal and the central provinces. The sepoys first rioted in Meerut and murdered their officers. They then marched on Delhi, which they captured and set up a descendant of the Great Mogul as emperor. Cawnpore was then taken by the rebels under Nana Sahib. Men, women and children were murdered and their bodies thrown into a well – only four escaped. The town was finally taken by Sir Colin Campbell. At Lucknow Sir Henry Lawrence held out at the residency for eighty-seven days. General Havelock and Sir James Outram relieved him, but he died soon after and they were themselves besieged until relieved by Campbell. Delhi was stormed by General Wilson and General Nicholson, who was killed in the ferocious fighting, during which the Cashmere gate was blown up. The second relief of Lucknow brought the mutiny to an end.

The East India Company lost control of India which was transferred to the crown and Victoria was proclaimed empress. A viceroy was appointed and acted through a minister in the British government. A council of men experienced in Indian affairs was named to advise the minister and India settled down peaceably under the new arrangements, though it would be true to say that the mutiny was really crushed because so many of the Indian princes remained loyal.

The Victorian era saw the continuation of colonising, begun in the Elizabethan age. In Canada there were troubles between Quebec and Ontario and Lord Durham was sent out to see what should be done. He advised the government to join the provinces together under a government modelled on the Westminster style. This was done and an act created the Dominion of Canada and a governor-general represented the queen in the country.

In Australia convicts had long been sent to Botany Bay. In 1851 gold was discovered in Victoria and soon each of the four Australian colonies was given government. In the next year the same thing was done in New Zealand. The system of transporting convicts to these countries was stopped from 1840 onwards. In New Zealand the Maoris accepted Victoria as their queen.

The Sudan, south of Egypt, had fallen into the hands of a fanatic called the Mahdi. General Gordon was sent out to organise the withdrawal of troops stationed there. He reached Khartoum but found himself besieged by the Mahdi. Sir Garnet Wolseley was sent out to relieve him, but arrived too late, for Khartoum was taken and General Gordon murdered. Twelve years later Sir Herbert Kitchener advanced up the Nile and defeated the Mahdi at Omdurman. This battle is also of interest as the last cavalry charge in army history took place at it and also because Winston Churchill was present as a civilian war correspondent.

In 1814 the Cape of South Africa had been bought from Holland. Some of the inhabitants in this area, Dutch Boers, emigrated and settled in what is now Natal. They wanted to make this area into an independent state, but British troops were moved in and so the Boers crossed the Vaal River and established the South African Republic, which the British government acknowledged. Gold and diamonds were discovered and large numbers of British and other nationalities came to make their fortunes. The Boers refused to grant them any rights and an armed force under Dr Jameson advanced to Johannesburg to their help. Jameson was compelled to surrender. We shall return to the story of South Africa towards the end of Victoria's reign.

Meanwhile, in the United States civil war broke out in 1861. This was a dreadful contest between the North or Federal States and the South or Confederate States and lasted four years, with very high casualties. The war began over the issue of keeping the Union together. The South wished to become independent of the North because it depended on slavery to run the tobacco, cotton and sugar plantations, but Northern opponents of slavery had obtained a majority in Congress. President Lincoln was determined to hold the Union together, but during the war proposed freedom for all slaves. The North eventually won this bloodiest of all wars and overran the South, abolishing slavery. This victory was due to the determination of the president and the military skill of General Grant. Lincoln did not live to see the results of his victory because he was assassinated by John Wilkes Booth, an out-of-work actor, in a theatre in Washington.

In Britain the Industrial Revolution had produced a vast increase in the population, through improvements in medicine and standards of living, and this resulted in overcrowding in the larger cities which developed. The Church of England and the non-conformist churches started missions in these cities. William Booth founded the Salvation Army and became its first general. He was formerly a Wesleyan preacher and he and his army carried religion and help into the very poorest districts.

One result of this concern for the poor was the rise of socialism. Karl Marx had produced a book, which he had written in the British Museum, suggesting that the property-owning and landed classes should disappear. The early trade unions took up this idea in the late eighties of the century and the Fabians, a group of British socialists, proposed that socialism should be introduced, but it made little progress until the dock strike of 1889. The dockers behaved in a very orderly manner which brought them great sympathy with the public. As a result, the trade union movement, which up to now had been illegal, was declared by the government to be legal.

Now we must return to South Africa, where the situation had not improved. As a result of the Jameson raid, the 'Uitlanders' or Outlanders, those who had come in search of gold and diamonds, were restricted even further in their rights. The Boers demanded an end to British sovereignty in return for a grant of voting powers to the Outlanders. Britain refused and declared war. Each side underestimated the other. The Boers did not realise the great power which Britain could eventually bring to bear and the British did not realise how skilful the Boers would prove to be in irregular warfare.

The Boers invaded Natal but were driven back and then besieged Ladysmith, but were unable to capture it. They also besieged Kimberley and Mafeking and three British defeats followed. General Gatacre was defeated at Stamberg, General Methuen at Magersfontein and General Buller at Colenso. They were attempting to relieve the three besieged towns. Enormous numbers of reinforcements were sent to the Cape under General Roberts, with Lord Kitchener as chief of staff. Victories soon followed and Mafeking was relieved, along with the other two besieged towns. Mafeking had been successfully defended by Colonel Baden-Powell, the founder of the Scout movement, for 215 days. General Roberts entered Pretoria and took over the Transvaal. Peace was signed in 1902.

During the war the longest reign so far in British history came to an end. Queen Victoria had celebrated two jubilees, one in 1887 and another ten years later. She had become a legend in her own lifetime and had survived Prince Albert by forty years. At her death on 22 January 1901 her descendants reigned over or were connected with nine European countries and she had earned the title of 'Grand Mother of Europe', but towards the end of the nineteenth century her strength began to weaken and she tired rapidly, dying at Osborne House on the Isle of Wight at the beginning of the twentieth century.

Chapter VIII

TWO WORLD WARS

Before moving to the First World War, there are some interesting social points to look at which took place during the Liberal government of 1906. Several extensions were made to the labour laws improving the position of the trade union movement. Employees were compelled by law to give compensation to injured workers. The army was reorganised and the first Dreadnought battleship was launched. Old-age pensions were introduced at five shillings (twenty-five pence) and labour exchanges were set up. A budget was introduced taxing large incomes to pay for social reforms and for increased naval expenditure. This led to the House of Lords rejecting the budget, but a general election returned the government and the budget resolutions were passed.

A group of women called suffragettes agitated for the right to vote. Up to now only men had been given this right. Led by Mrs Pankhurst they smashed windows and invaded the House of Commons. When arrested they went on hunger strike, chained themselves to Downing Street railings and refused to pay any fines. Votes were given to all women over thirty in 1918 and to those over twenty-one in 1928. These early years of the century, usually called the Edwardian age, after Edward VII, are looked back on as an age of peace and prosperity, but many could see the beginnings of the decline of the British Empire and the rise of a new aggressive spirit in Germany under Kaiser Wilhelm II which was to lead in 1914 to the First World War.

The reasons for the war were far-reaching. Germany and Britain had been rivals for a long time over African colonisation and for naval and trading superiority. Since 1870, when the French lost to Germany, there had been a desire on the French side for revenge. In the Balkans, Austria and Russia had long been competing for influence. Two hostile groups had formed during these years. Germany, Austria and Italy were one group; France, Russia and Britain were the other. Italy broke from their alliance during the war. Something had to happen to make these groups fight and that occurred in June 1914. The heir to the Austro-Hungarian throne, Archduke Ferdinand, and his wife, Archduchess Sophie, were murdered at Sarajevo in Bosnia. Austria invaded Serbia and Russia came to the help of the Serbs. Germany declared war on Russia and France and invaded Belgium. Britain ordered Germany to withdraw from Belgium and, when they did not, war was declared.

During 1914 the Allies were driven back to the River Marne and the war settled down in the West to trench warfare. On the eastern front the Russians were heavily defeated by the Germans at Tannenburg. The second year of the war produced enormous casualty rates in the trenches for small gains or losses amounting to only a few yards. British, Australian and New Zealand forces attempted a diversionary attack on the Gallipoli Peninsula which ultimately failed. At sea a small British fleet was defeated at the Coronel, but later won a victory off the Falkland Isles.

In 1916 the only major sea battle of the war took place off Jutland. Neither side was really willing to be fully involved with the other so the battle was indecisive. The British commander was Admiral Jellicoe and he was keen to protect his fleet as he knew that if he was defeated the war could easily be lost. The British lost fourteen ships to the Germans' eleven, and German gunnery showed itself to be more accurate than the British. Both sides claimed victory, but the German navy returned to base and stayed there for the remainder of the war.

'Jack' Cornwell was posthumously awarded the Victoria Cross at the age of sixteen for extreme gallantry at the Battle of Jutland. Despite being mortally wounded he remained standing alone at his post by his gun, waiting for orders, while the gun crew lay dead or wounded round him. The German naval command now turned to unrestricted submarine warfare. On the western front both sides continued large-scale attacks with huge losses. At the Battle of the Somme, the British advanced nine miles at a cost of over four hundred thousand casualties.

In 1917 German submarine warfare was proving very effective, and their attempt to starve Britain was having serious consequences, but the sinking of American ships – especially the *Lusitania* full of American citizens – by German submarines brought the USA into the war on the Allied side.

In Russia revolution took place and Tsar Nicholas abdicated. The new Bolshevik government signed an armistice with Germany. In what was otherwise a very black year for the British and the Allies, General Allenby captured Jerusalem. This was the culmination of the campaign which Lawrence of Arabia had led. On the western front the high losses continued and small gains were made in the mud at Ypres with appalling casualties. Tanks first appeared at the Battle of Cambrai.

In 1918 Allied naval superiority was used to blockade the central European powers and the Americans poured reinforcements onto the battlefields in the west.

The Germans brought their troops from the Russian front to try to force an immediate victory and were successful at first. Marshal Foch was appointed to the supreme Allied command and held the Germans at the Battle of the Marne and in July attacked them. During the next four months the Allied offensive drove the Germans back and an armistice was signed on 11 November. The Kaiser fled to Holland, where he stayed for the rest of his long life, dying there in 1941.

The war left both sides exhausted, but peace treaties had to be signed. By the terms Germany lost Alsace-Lorraine to France and some territory to the new Polish Republic. The Austro-Hungarian Empire was split up, with independence given to Hungary, Czechoslovakia and some of the Balkan states under the new name of Yugoslavia. The Turkish Empire was also broken up. Iraq and Saudi Arabia became independent monarchical states. The Baltic republics of Latvia, Estonia, Lithuania and Finland were re-established. Germany lost its African colonies and its navy surrendered, only to scuttle itself in Scapa Flow. The new German Republic was ordered to pay vast sums of money to the Allies, thereby sowing the seeds of the Second World War. On the suggestion of President Wilson the League of Nations was set up. Unfortunately, he could not persuade Congress that the USA should be a member, so it never had the world influence that it might have had with American participation.

Between the two world wars we have a period often called the 'Rise of the Dictators' and it is true that the thirties were dominated by Hitler and Mussolini. However, before discussing why the Second World War broke out, we should look at some other points.

The years after the First World War were difficult ones. The miners went on strike for higher wages in 1921. Unemployment rose, contrary to the promises of the wartime government, and by 1926 conditions in the mining areas were causing real hardship. In this year a General Strike was called but the government, under Stanley Baldwin, was ready and the TUC was defeated.

The Labour party took office for the first time in 1924, but was dependent on Liberal support and did not last for long. It was returned in 1929 but again with not enough seats to form a majority government, and as the country and indeed most of the world was hit by a financial crisis and depression, a national government was formed under Ramsay MacDonald.

Meanwhile Benito Mussolini had taken office in Italy and Adolf Hitler in Germany. Conditions in both countries were poor. In Germany this was a direct result of the enormous amount of money the Allies had demanded from the German people to pay for the cost of the war. In the Far East Japan sought to enlarge its influence and invaded Manchuria, and in Africa Italy invaded Ethiopia. This was in 1935 and Britain began to rearm.

In 1936 the British royal family was very much in the news when Edward VIII abdicated and was succeeded by George VI. The new king went on a highly successful tour of North America and re-established the position of the monarchy in this country very quickly.

Stanley Baldwin gave way to Neville Chamberlain in 1937. The Chamberlain government tried to remove the German threat by a policy of concessions – known as appeasement – but to no avail. In 1938 Germany took over Austria and the next year marched into Czechoslovakia.

Germany had suffered greatly both during and after the First World War and wanted revenge. Hitler and his National Socialist

Party, the Nazis, seemed to satisfy the desires of many Germans, and by 1933 he was chancellor, then later Führer. Under Hitler the Rhineland was re-fortified.

Hitler and Mussolini met and made an agreement and then made another with Russia in 1939. Fine new roads were built in Germany, designed for swift movement of the military, and conscription was introduced and the German army rearmed. War began to look inevitable, as indeed Winston Churchill and others said publicly. Britain guaranteed Polish neutrality early in 1939. On 1 September Germany invaded Poland and was immediately told to withdraw. This Germany refused to do and on Sunday, 3 September 1939, Neville Chamberlain broadcast to the people, telling them that Britain and France were again at war with Germany, only twenty-one years after the end of the First World War. Europe was once again living up to its reputation of trying to settle its disputes by war.

The German Panzer tank divisions rapidly conquered Western Poland. Russia invaded from the east and Poland was divided between the two countries. A British Expeditionary Force was sent to France, but no major battles were fought. Meanwhile, on the east coast of South America, the German pocket battleship, *Graf Spee*, was compelled to run for shelter in the River Plate and there scuttled itself on the orders of Hitler.

Early in 1940 Germany overran in quick succession Denmark, Norway, Holland and Belgium. The British Expeditionary Force advanced to the help of the Belgians but was cut off by a rapid German advance into France and forced to withdraw at Dunkirk, leaving most of its equipment behind. France signed an armistice and General de Gaulle rallied French resistance from London. Italy attacked Greece and British troops were sent to Greece, but the Germans invaded and Britain withdrew.

Neville Chamberlain resigned and Winston Churchill became prime minister. Germany tried to destroy the Royal Air Force in the Battle of Britain in preparation for invasion, but failed and turned instead to night bombing of London and other cities. The Germans also used submarine warfare effectively.

In 1941 it became clear that America under President Roosevelt was gradually abandoning its neutral position and in March

Congress allowed defence materials, in particular shipping, to be transferred to Britain. In Europe Germany invaded Yugoslavia, but then Hitler attempted to do what Napoleon had tried and failed. He attacked Russia. The Russian forces were driven rapidly back, but held the German line before Moscow. Then in December the Americans were suddenly attacked by the Japanese at Pearl Harbor and joined the Allies against the central European powers. Peace terms were being discussed at the time of the attack.

In 1942 the Japanese advanced rapidly in the South Pacific. hey overran Hong Kong, the Philippines, many South Pacific Islands, Malaya, Singapore and Burma, but were unable to invade India. Allied resources had to be sent to the Pacific. In this area the tide of war began to turn slowly and there were naval victories for the Allies at Coral Sea and the Midway Islands. In North Africa British forces under General Wavell defeated the Italians and advanced into Libya but were forced back by the Germans under Rommel. Later in the year the Eighth Army under General Montgomery was re-formed and defeated Rommel in a ten-day battle at El Alamein. Rommel retreated rapidly along the North African coast. In Russia the German advance continued as far as Stalingrad. Here it ground to a halt and the winter offensive destroyed the German army besieging the city. The tide of war had now turned in all sectors.

German resistance in North Africa ended in May 1943 and the Allies invaded Sicily. As Allied forces landed in Italy Mussolini fell from power and an armistice with Italy was signed. The German forces in Italy built strong defences in the north of the country and slowed the Allied advance. In Russia the Russian army was now able to turn on the offensive on a very long front from the Baltic to the Crimea. In Europe the Allies increased their bombing attacks on German cities. The Americans began to recapture many South Pacific Islands and early in 1944 landed in the Philippines.

In the same year the British recaptured Burma reaching the Chindwin River. This British army was under the command of General Slim. The Russians continued their advance and Romania surrendered. The Baltic states were freed, as was Finland. In Italy Rome was taken. On 6 June the Allies under General Eisenhower landed in Normandy.

After fierce fighting British forces wore down the German units around Caen and the Americans broke through. Paris was freed in August and the Germans driven out of France. An attempt to cross the Rhine at Arnhem failed and a German counter-attack in the Ardennes in winter was met and defeated. The Germans launched rockets at Britain. The year 1945 began with fanatical fighting from the Japanese in the Pacific, but their forces in Okinawa and Burma were destroyed. The Russians marched into Austria and the Allies crossed the Rhine at Remagen. Russian and Allied troops met on the Elbe and Hitler committed suicide as the Russians attacked Berlin. On 7 May Hitler's successor, Admiral Dönitz, ordered the unconditional surrender of all German troops. Allied attacks on Japan increased and in August an atom bomb was dropped on Hiroshima. Three days later another was dropped on Nagasaki. Japan surrendered and the Second World War was over.

Chapter IX

THE PRESENT DAY

Since the Second World War communications around the world have improved so much that we can now see history being made. There is therefore much more to be chosen from and so we must be selective. Our selection is as follows.

In Britain for the first time a Labour government was returned with a large majority, able to carry out a wide programme. This was the beginning of the welfare state, though it is true to say that many of the ideas had appeared during the war. Comprehensive National Insurance was brought in and the National Health Service was established. Coal mines, road and rail transport, electricity and gas were nationalised and education reformed.

In Europe the Nuremberg Trials were held and several Nazi war criminals executed. The USA provided large amounts of help for Europe under the Marshall Plan. India was granted independence and fighting broke out between Jews and Arabs in Palestine. Several European countries established economic union and the North Atlantic Treaty Organisation was set up.

The Labour government of Clement Attlee was returned in 1950, but lost power the next year and Churchill became prime minister again. George VI died in 1952 and his daughter became queen as Elizabeth II. In 1947 she had married Prince Philip of Greece and they had had two children by the time of her accession, Prince Charles and Princess Anne.

The state of Israel was established in 1948 and in several wars showed itself superior to its neighbours. Troubles in that area still continue. In 1956 Egypt, under President Nasser, nationalised the Suez Canal. Britain and France attempted to keep the canal open, but were not supported by America in the United Nations and had to withdraw. The British dismantled their empire too rapidly and this caused problems in many African states who were not ready for self-government, though they demanded and were given it.

The Americans under United Nations authority were involved in wars in Korea and South Vietnam. The latter led to American withdrawal from that area and a loss of American pride. This self-esteem was not to return until the time of the Gulf War.

The cold war between the West and the East continued through the Berlin blockade of 1948 and through the Cuban crisis. In fact, the cold war has only recently come to an end with the collapse of Soviet domination in Eastern Europe and the destruction of the Berlin wall.

It can easily be seen from these last few paragraphs that we have left the study of history and have been looking at current affairs. We will, therefore, close here and hope that the reader will now study the history of this land in more detail for we have only shown the outlines of our history and there is much more to be discovered by the interested reader.

Appendix I

CHRONOLOGY

55–54 BC	Julius Caesar invaded Britain
AD 43	Claudius invaded Britain
60	Boudicca' s rebellion
122–127	Building of Hadrian's Wall
410	Traditional date of Romans leaving Britain
597	St Augustine landed in Kent
664	Synod of Whitby
871–899	Alfred
878	Treaty of Wedmore
1066	Battle of Hastings. Battle of Stamford Bridge
	William I
1086	Domesday Book (survey result)
1087	William II
1100	Henry I
1135	Stephen
1154	Henry II
1170	Murder of Archbishop Becket
1189	Richard I
1190–1192	Third crusade
1199	John
1214	Battle of Bouvines. John expelled from France
1215	Magna Carta. Archbishop Langton
1216	Henry III
1265	Model Parliament
	Battle of Evesham. De Montfort killed
1272	Edward I
1307	Edward II
1314	Battle of Bannockbum
1327	Edward III

1340	Battle of Sluys
1346	Battle of Crécy
1348–1349	Black Death
1356	Battle of Poitiers
1360	Treaty of Brétigny
1377	Richard II
1381	Peasants' Revolt
1399	Henry IV
1413	Henry V
1415	Battle of Agincourt
1431	Joan of Arc burnt at Rouen
1455	Wars of the Roses began
1461	Edward IV
1483	Edward V
	Richard III
1485	Henry VII
	Battle of Bosworth. Last battle of the Wars of the Roses
1492	Columbus discovered America
1509	Henry VIII
1529	Dismissal of Wolsey
1547	Edward VI
1549	The First Prayer Book
1553	Mary I
1558	Loss of Calais
	Elizabeth I
1587	Execution of Mary, Queen of Scots
1588	Spanish Armada
1603	James I
1605	Gunpowder Plot
1611	Authorised Version of the Bible
1625	Charles I
1642	Outbreak of the English Civil War
1649	Execution of Charles I
1658	Death of Oliver Cromwell
1660	Restoration of Charles II
1665	Great Plague
1666	Great Fire

1685	James II
	Battle of Sedgemoor
1688	Glorious Revolution. Trial of the seven bishops
1689	William III and Mary II
1694	Bank of England obtained a charter
1702	Anne
1704	Battle of Blenheim. Marlborough
1707	Union of Scottish and English Parliaments
1714	George I
1715	First Jacobite rebellion led by the Old Pretender, son of James II
1720	South Sea Bubble
1727	George II
1745	Second Jacobite rebellion led by Bonnie Prince Charlie, son of Old Pretender
1757	Battle of Plassey. Clive in India
1759	Capture of Quebec. Wolfe in Quebec
1760	George III
1776	Declaration of American independence
1789	Fall of the Bastille. Outbreak of French Revolution
1805	Battle of Trafalgar. Nelson
1815	Battle of Waterloo. Wellington
1820	George IV
1830	William IV
1832	Great Reform Bill
1837	Victoria
1846	Repeal of the Corn Laws
1854–1856	Crimean War. Florence Nightingale
1857–1858	Indian Mutiny
1887	Golden Jubilee of Queen Victoria
1897	Diamond Jubilee of Queen Victoria
1899–1902	Boer War. Roberts and Kitchener
1901	Edward VII
1904	Entente Cordiale between France and England
1910	George V
1914–1918	First World War
1916	Battle of Jutland. Jellicoe. Battle of the Somme
1919	Treaty of Versailles

1922	Mussolini established Fascism in Italy
1924	First Labour government
1926	General Strike
1933	Hitler established Nazism in Germany
1935	Italy invaded Abyssinia
1936	Edward VIII
	George VI
	Spanish Civil War. Franco
1939–1945	Second World War
1940	Battle of Britain
1941	Japanese attack on Pearl Harbor
1945	Labour government under Clement Attlee
1946	Sir Winston Churchill's 'Iron Curtain' speech at Fulton. Nuremberg Trials
1947	Marriage of Princess Elizabeth and Prince Philip of Greece
1948	Assassination of Gandhi. Marshall Plan
	Foundation of the state of Israel. Berlin Blockade
1949	NATO treaty signed
1950	China occupied Tibet. Korean War
1951	Churchill PM again
1952	Elizabeth II
1953	Death of Stalin
1954	Battle of Dien Bien Phu. Peace in Indo-China
1955	Italy, West Germany and France established European Union
1956	Suez campaign. USSR invaded Hungary
1957	Beginning of Common Market
1958	De Gaulle elected president of France
1961	John F Kennedy became president of the USA
1963	Kennedy assassinated
1964	Harold Wilson PM. Vietnam War
1965	Winston Churchill died
1966	Mrs Indira Gandhi became prime minister of India
1967	Six-day war between Israel and the Arabs
1968	USSR invaded Czechoslovakia
1969	Beginning of the present Ulster troubles
1970	Edward Heath PM

1973	Britain joined the Common Market
1974	Harold Wilson PM. Watergate scandal in the USA
	Resignation of President Nixon
1979	Mrs Margaret Thatcher PM
1981	Marriage of Prince Charles and Princess Diana
1982	Falklands campaign. Birth of Prince William
1989	Destruction of the Berlin Wall
1990	Gulf campaign

SAXON KINGS OF ENGLAND

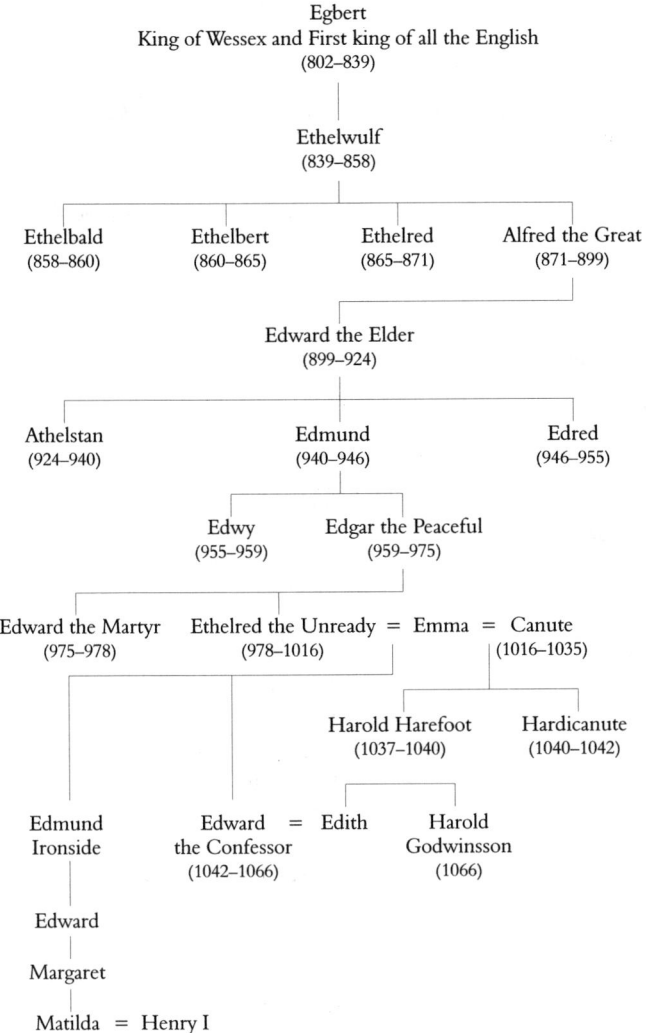

Egbert
King of Wessex and First king of all the English
(802–839)

Ethelwulf
(839–858)

Ethelbald
(858–860)

Ethelbert
(860–865)

Ethelred
(865–871)

Alfred the Great
(871–899)

Edward the Elder
(899–924)

Athelstan
(924–940)

Edmund
(940–946)

Edred
(946–955)

Edwy
(955–959)

Edgar the Peaceful
(959–975)

Edward the Martyr
(975–978)

Ethelred the Unready = Emma = Canute
(978–1016)   (1016–1035)

Harold Harefoot
(1037–1040)

Hardicanute
(1040–1042)

Edmund
Ironside

Edward = Edith
the Confessor
(1042–1066)

Harold
Godwinsson
(1066)

Edward

Margaret

Matilda = Henry I

NORMAN AND PLANTAGENET

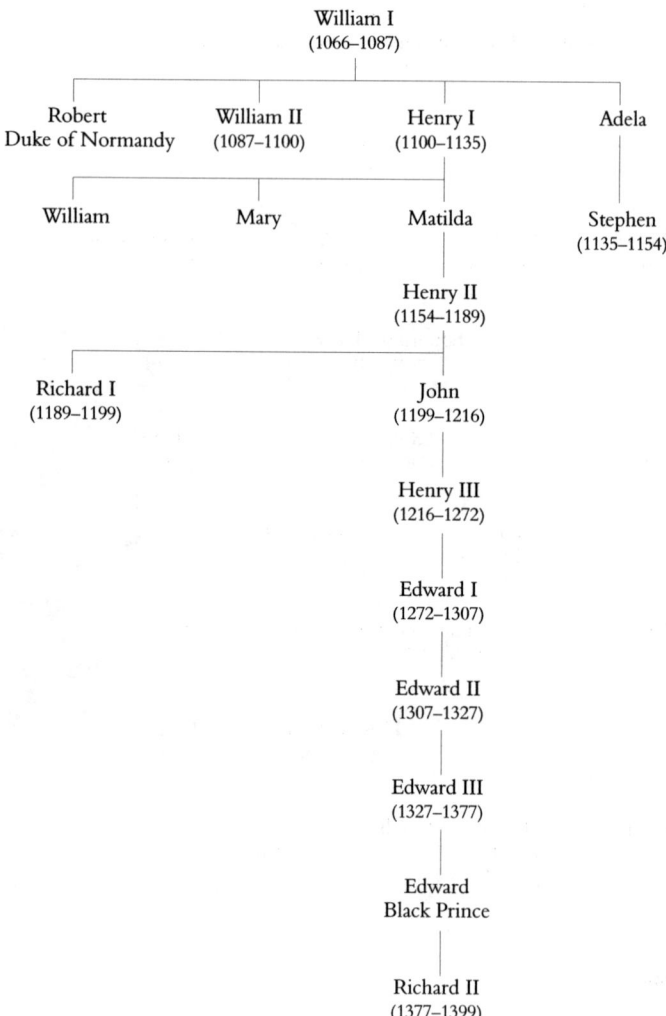

YORK AND LANCASTER

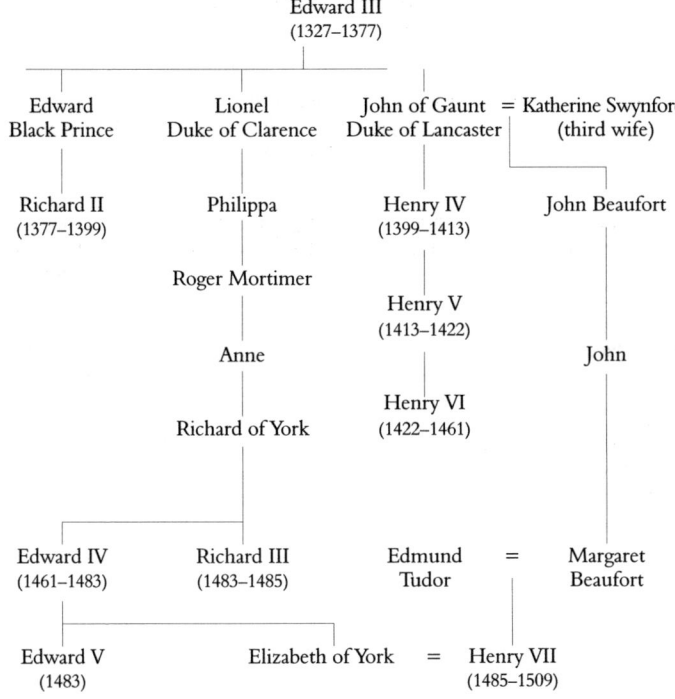

TUDOR

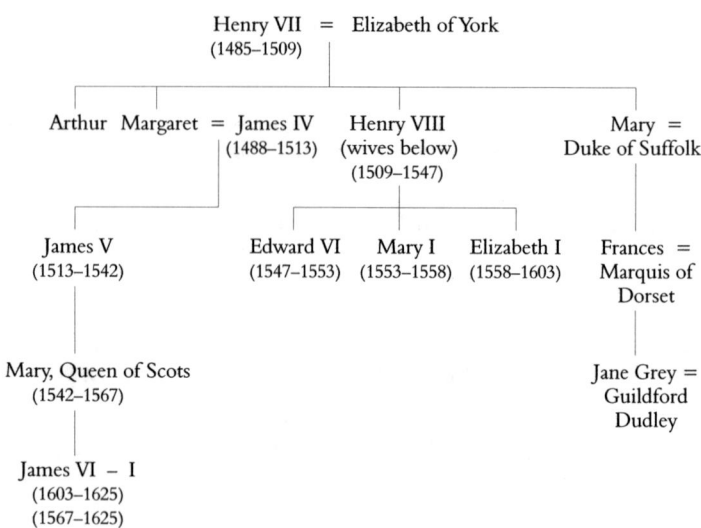

Wives of Henry VIII:

1	Catherine of Aragon	Divorced
2	Anne Boleyn	Beheaded
3	Jane Seymour	Died
4	Anne of Cleves	Divorced
5	Catherine Howard	Beheaded
6	Catherine Parr	Survived

STUART AND HANOVERIAN

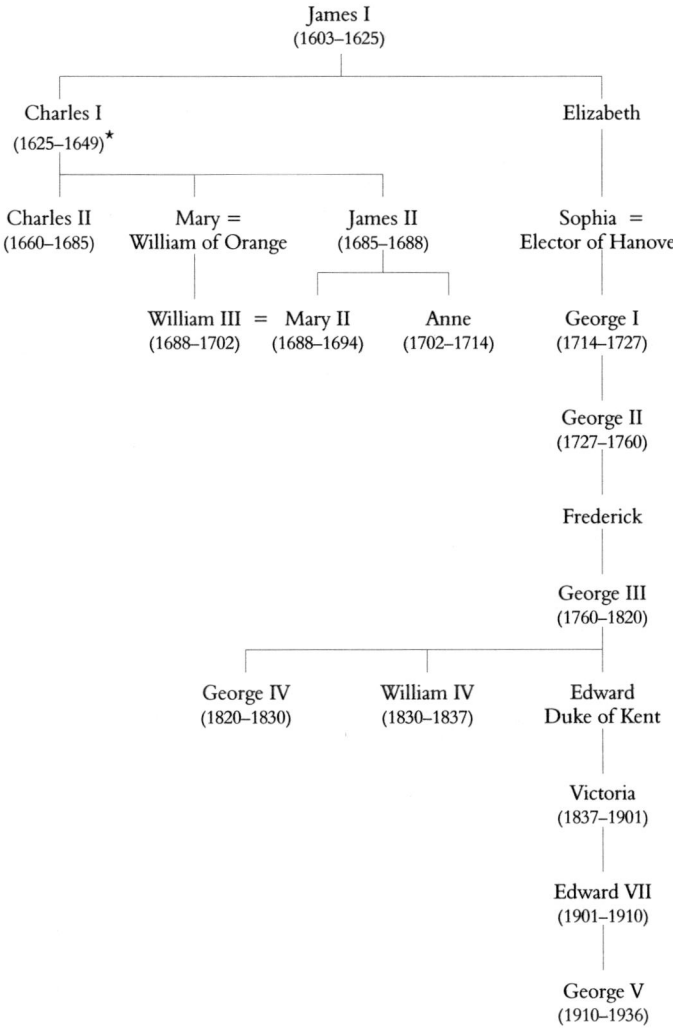

James I
(1603–1625)

Charles I
(1625–1649)★

Elizabeth

Charles II
(1660–1685)

Mary =
William of Orange

James II
(1685–1688)

Sophia =
Elector of Hanover

William III = Mary II
(1688–1702) (1688–1694)

Anne
(1702–1714)

George I
(1714–1727)

George II
(1727–1760)

Frederick

George III
(1760–1820)

George IV
(1820–1830)

William IV
(1830–1837)

Edward
Duke of Kent

Victoria
(1837–1901)

Edward VII
(1901–1910)

George V
(1910–1936)

★ Commonwealth of Oliver Cromwell (1649–1660)

WINDSOR*

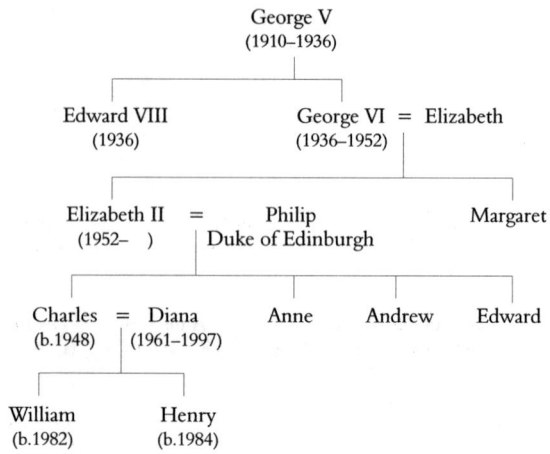

George V
(1910–1936)

Edward VIII   George VI = Elizabeth
(1936)   (1936–1952)

Elizabeth II = Philip   Margaret
(1952–)   Duke of Edinburgh

Charles = Diana   Anne   Andrew   Edward
(b.1948)   (1961–1997)

William   Henry
(b.1982)   (b.1984)

* Changed to Windsor in 1917